THE MAKING OF
STAR TREK ®
FIRST CONTACT ™

THE MAKING OF
STAR TREK®
FIRST CONTACT™

LOU ANDERS

ADDITIONAL MATERIAL BY LARRY NEMECEK & IAN SPELLING

TITAN BOOKS

THE MAKING OF STAR TREK: FIRST CONTACT
ISBN 1 85286 779 5

Published by
Titan Books
42-44 Dolben Street
London SE1 0UP

First edition December 1996
10 9 8 7 6 5 4 3 2 1

British Library Cataloguing-in-Publication Data. A catalogue record for this book is available from the British Library.

Design by Chris Teather.
Production by Bob Kelly.

DEDICATION:

The author would like to thank Kristin Torgen, without whom this book would not have been possible. Thanks are also due to Marsha Anders, Brannon Braga, Jonathan Frakes and John Freeman.

The publishers would like to thank Jon Hipps, Margaret Clark and Marco Palmieri at Pocket Books, Paula M. Block at Paramount, Larry Nemecek and Ian Spelling, and all the cast and crew of *Star Trek: First Contact*, for their tireless help with this project.

Star Trek: First Contact photos by John Eaves, Elliot Marks and Industrial Light & Magic.

For a complete list of all Titan's *Star Trek* publications, please send a large stamped SAE to Titan Books Mail Order, PO Box 54, Desborough, Northants, NN14 2UH. You can also order any title from the same address, or telephone 01536 763 631 with your credit card details. Please quote MSTFC.

Printed and bound in Great Britain by Stephens and George Ltd, Merthyr Industrial Estate, Dowlais, Merthyr Tydfil.

CONTENTS

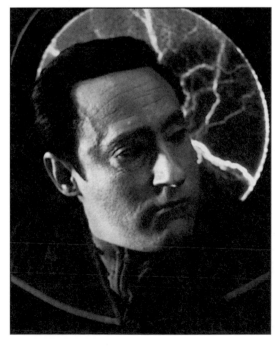

Thirty years ago, on 8 September 1966, Gene Roddenberry's *Star Trek* aired on television for the first time. Though the series only lasted three seasons, it quickly became a cult favourite in syndication and achieved a popularity in reruns beyond that of any other science fiction series. Over time, the images of its heroes, most notably Captain Kirk, Mr. Spock and Doctor McCoy, have become part and parcel of our culture, charac-

ters in an ongoing fictional universe that many regard as nothing less than modern mythology.

In 1975, Gene Roddenberry and Paramount Pictures were in serious talks to develop *Star Trek: Phase II*, a new television series continuing the adventures of the original crew. As work got underway, two things happened to change the plans for a second television series. Firstly, potential sponsors were uninterested in backing another science fiction series. Secondly, the twofold success of *Star Wars* and *Close Encounters of the Third Kind* in the cinema was impossible to ignore. Paramount subsequently announced it would turn *Star Trek* into a major motion picture.

In 1979, *Star Trek: The Motion Picture* premiered. Though the film was not a critical success, it was enough of a box office hit to warrant a sequel. *Star Trek: The Motion Picture* launched the full original series

NING . . . .

crew into five subsequent movies. Of all of the films, *Star Trek II: The Wrath of Khan* emerged as a standard against which the others would always be compared, a triumphant blend of exciting space action with real human themes of death and fleeting youth.

Following the success of *The Wrath of Khan*, further movies appeared at roughly two year intervals. *Star Trek III: The Search for Spock* and *Star Trek IV: The Voyage Home* were both directed by Leonard Nimoy, the latter gaining Oscar nominations for Don Peterman's cinematography and Leonard Rosenman's music. For the fifth feature, *Star Trek V: The Final Frontier*, another *Star Trek* actor took the helm: William Shatner. These adventures saw Captain Kirk dealing with issues of ageing and mortality, while Captain Spock came to accept his own humanity. Along the way, they saved the Earth a few times as well.

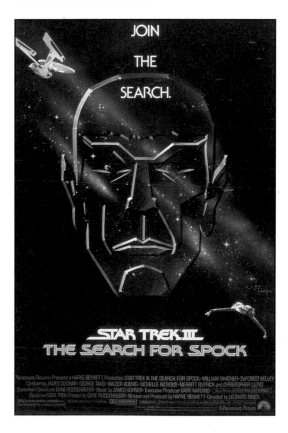

While all this was going on at the cinema, Gene Roddenberry launched his second *Star Trek* series, *Star Trek: The Next Generation*. Premiering in 1987, it took place on the *Enterprise*-D, seventy-eight years farther into the future. Original series stars DeForest Kelley, James Doohan and Leonard Nimoy all appeared in episodes, their presence providing a connection with the past. First seen as the new kid on the block and subjected to unfair comparisons,

The Next Generation swiftly emerged as *the Star Trek* for a whole new generation of television viewers.

In 1991, the sixth film in the franchise, *Star Trek VI: The Undiscovered Country*, appeared on the twenty-fifth anniversary of the original series. It was a wonderful farewell to the entire original cast. In a fictionalised mirror of real events occurring between the Soviet Union and America, *The Undiscovered Country* saw the end of hostilities between the Feder-

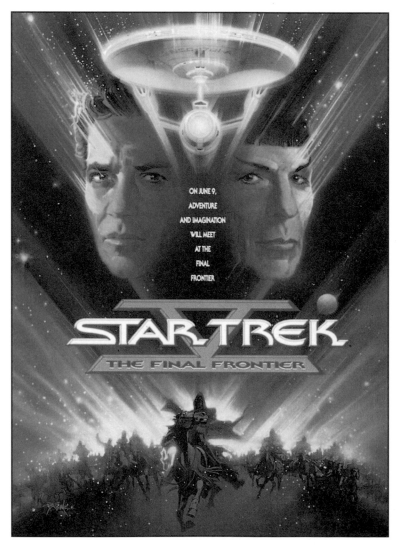

ation and the Klingon Empire, as Captain Kirk was reluctantly forced to carry the banner of peace to his greatest enemies. Beautifully directed by Nicholas Meyer, *The Undiscovered Country* incorporated all of the best elements of the original series. It also included, as a cameo tailored for fans of *The Next Generation*, an appearance by Michael Dorn. His role, the Klingon trial lawyer assigned to defend Kirk and McCoy, had a familiar name: Worf. Playing the grandfather of his character in *The Next Generation*, Dorn was the first of the new batch of *Star Trek* actors to appear in the film franchise, a sound link between one generation and the next.

In 1994, after seven seasons, *The Next Generation* itself went off the air, having successfully launched its own spin-off, *Star Trek: Deep Space Nine,* which was later joined by *Star Trek: Voyager*. Soon after their departure from television, *The Next Generation* cast returned in their first big screen adventure, *Star Trek*

Now, two years later, on the thirtieth anniversary of the first *Star Trek* episode, the stage is set for the first ever *Star Trek* film to feature solely *The Next Generation* crew, as the cast reunites on the bridge of a new *Enterprise*. Now they face the greatest peril in Federation history, an enemy bent on the conquest of Earth and the destruction of Starfleet history — the Borg. ∎

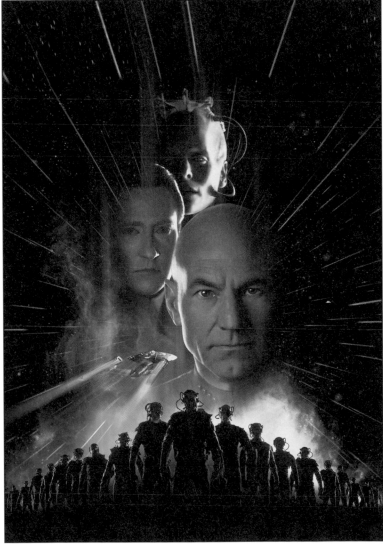

Generations. The film begins in the twenty-third century at the launch of the *Enterprise*-B, with Kirk, Scotty and Chekov as the honoured celebrities at the ceremony. An emergency requires the new *Enterprise* to spring into action even though the final construction of the starship is not yet complete. An explosion caused by an encounter with a strange phenomenon called the Nexus results in the apparent death of Captain Kirk. Years later, the crew of the *Enterprise*-D again come up against the Nexus. Picard is swept into it, only to find Kirk there as well. The two captains emerge to save the day, their meeting viewed as the official 'passing of the baton' from the original *Star Trek* to *Star Trek: The Next Generation*. When Kirk dies at the film's climax, the torch really has been passed from one era to another. *Star Trek Generations* also saw one of the most exciting sequences in all of the *Star Trek* films, the destruction of the *Enterprise*-D and the emergency crash-landing of its detachable saucer section.

PRE-PRODUCTION

The Borg were central to the ideas that screenwriters Brannon Braga and Ronald D. Moore had for Star Trek: First Contact.

tar Trek: First Contact Producer Rick Berman has steadfastly guided an ever-growing *Star Trek* universe. He produced *Star Trek Generations*, was executive producer of *Star Trek: The Next Generation* and is currently co-creator/executive producer of both *Star Trek: Voyager* and *Star Trek: Deep Space Nine*. Early in 1995 Berman approached *Star Trek Generations* screenwriters Brannon Braga and Ronald D. Moore about the next *Star Trek* feature.

"It was an open book," says Braga. "The only dictum was make this a *Star Trek: The Next Generation* adventure only." As Moore explains, "At the very beginning, which was somewhere around February or March of 1995, Rick started talking about the next

picture to Brannon and me. Rick wanted to do a time travel picture, and he wasn't sure what the story would be, or who it would involve. Brannon and I wanted to do a picture about the Borg and do a big action thing. Basically, we just married those two ideas."

The Borg had attempted the assimilation of Earth once before and been defeated by the Federation. It therefore seemed a natural leap of logic that the Borg might try to undermine their opponents by defeating the Earth before there *was* a Federation. "Their whole thing is to assimilate humanity and destroy the future," explains Moore, "so if they can't beat us in the present, they'll go back in time and solve their problem."

Next up was the problem of choosing a time period. "We went through several," says Moore. "We talked extensively at one point about the Italian Renaissance, because we thought that would be a neat period where a lot of scientific discoveries were being made. Mankind was coming out of the dark age into an age of enlightenment. But ultimately, it just seemed too removed for the audience. It's a time period in which some of the costumes might be a problem. We didn't want to see everybody running around in tights, and so on. Part of me kind of wishes that we had tried it. Fighting the Borg, a highly technological race, in a low-tech environment is kind of cool. After that, we talked at various points about a lot of different points of history. We decided that most of it had been mined in one way or another by various time travel stories in science fiction and in *Star Trek*."

Eventually, the early twenty-first century was decided upon, a time which, according to the *Star Trek* canon, humankind was emerging from a second Dark Age into a new Renaissance. Braga explains the rationale behind bringing the Borg to the twenty-first century: "The Borg would turn to the most technologically advanced time with the least resistance. About sixty years from now, there will have been a third world war, and some scientist named Zefram Cochrane is about to develop warp drive. When he

Ron Moore on giving the Collective a Queen: *"One of the things with the Borg has always been the difficulty of dealing with a race that is decentralised dramatically, because there's no one thing to focus on, there's no character to go up against. It's hard to write scenes about us versus the Collective. We did try initially to go with the Collective as a collective and not establish a single villain, sort of like in* Aliens. *Even in that movie, they had to find the Big Mama eventually. We got to the point where we needed somebody to personify the Borg for us, somebody to hate, somebody to talk to, somebody to get an idea of where they're coming from and who, once they've destroyed you, would destroy everybody else. Also, we wanted something for Data. Data's arc, in which he discovered a part of humanity he hadn't anticipated through the acquisition of flesh, was something that was tailor made for the Queen. So we just started thinking about a leader of the Borg, and calling her the Borg Queen among ourselves."*

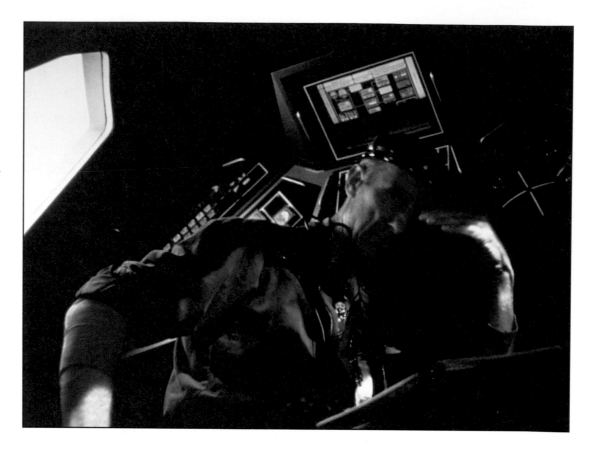

makes the first warp flight, this catches the eye of some passing Vulcans and they make first contact with Earth. That contact eventually leads to the formation of the Federation and Starfleet and within fifty years, humanity's 'star trek' is born. In a funny way what's at stake in this movie is *Star Trek* itself. If the Borg stop Cochrane from doing his first warp flight, the *Star Trek* universe will never come into existence."

From this springboard, the story began to take shape. "The initial drafts have Captain Picard down on the surface of the planet," explains Moore. "Picard goes to Earth to the missile silo, where Cochrane's ship is poised for its maiden flight. But the ship is damaged. Picard remains on the surface. Riker goes back to the *Enterprise*. On the surface of the planet Picard meets up with the character that's now called Lily, who in the early drafts was called Ruby. She is living in a town nearby, which is called Resurrection." At this point, the script was being referred to as *Star Trek: Resurrection* after the town, but that title was soon abandoned when it was announced that the fourth *Alien* feature would be called *Alien 4: Resurrection*.

In these early drafts, Picard is cut off from the *Enterprise* and has to repair the damaged ship's warp drive himself to preserve history. "Cochrane is unconscious for the entire movie," explains Braga.

"He basically gets blasted by the Borg and remains in Beverly's sickbay and doesn't wake up until the warp flight is already done."

"There were also some futuristic militia groups roaming the countryside," Moore recalls. "They became the villains down on the planet's surface

that Picard had to fight against. Picard basically did the launch himself, and flew the warp ship at the end of the movie." Meanwhile, 'upstairs' on the *Enterprise*, events began to unfold, with a Borg invasion force slowly assimilating the ship. In these early versions, it was Riker who fought to save the ship: "Riker and Worf are fighting the Borg on the *Enterprise*, culminating in the big spacewalk sequence that's in the picture now, and the Borg Queen storyline is going on at the same time with Data."

At that point, input from a lead actor and reservations on Braga and Moore's part led to a major breakthrough. "We had some discussions with Patrick about it." Moore reveals. "He had some reservations about the way the Ruby storyline was working on the planet's surface. He wasn't buying into the romance the way we had detailed it. We weren't too happy with the way the militia groups were working. Brannon, Rick and I thought that the militia group was becoming a very cardboard easy to knock down 'stick figure' for our heroes. It just wasn't quite gelling. We said, 'Wait a minute! This is about the Borg, for crying out loud, and it's weird that we have a picture where Picard is not dealing with the Borg, since he's the one character on the show who has the biggest backstory with them.'

"We went, 'Duh! What if we just swap Riker and Picard. Throw the emphasis 'upstairs', make the *Enterprise* story the primary story with Picard, put Riker down on the planet's surface and wake up Zefram Cochrane.' We could play that for more of a light adventure 'downstairs', forget about the militias and just make the B-story about dealing with the inventor from the past who's nothing like you thought he would be. Then go 'upstairs' and have Picard facing his greatest nightmare, which is that the Borg are back, they want him, and they want his ship. We still wanted the character Ruby, who's now called Lily, and we needed to get her onto the ship. That was really the last major conceptual jump; everything after that was pretty much as it is now."

With Cochrane 'awake', the character quickly

Brannon Braga on tempering down the Picard/Lily romance: "We tried it in the first draft. We gave it a shot, and it didn't work. They fell in love, and he took her to the future, and there was a wonderful romance for him. It didn't work, because you had a Picard who was falling in love in just a couple of days while the Borg were assimilating Earth, and the Captain would never do that. Even if we could believe that he could fall in love in a couple of days, which is implausible at best, he just wouldn't take the time to do that when the Borg are about to destroy the future. So we dropped it. But we wanted to retain the Lily character and we thought it would be more interesting to explore the difference between a person from the twenty-fourth century and a person from [nearly] our time [the mid twenty-first century]."

Right and opposite page: *Actor-director Jonathan Frakes helms his first feature film.* **Below:** *Patrick Stewart on set.*

wrote itself. "We realised in subsequent drafts that this is an interesting character," says Braga. "You kind of want to meet the guy. He's such a critical part of history. One of the things that we thought was an interesting idea was that if you went back in history, if you went back to meet one of your heroes like Abe Lincoln or the Wright Brothers, you might find meeting them in person, smelling the environment they lived in, and really just being there, very different from reading about it.

"We thought it would be cool if the man who basically ushered in a new era in humanity was motivated by things that were antithetical to *Star Trek*. There's something interesting about meeting a hero who not only is not what you expected, but has to fill the shoes that history said he would fill. Cochrane has to find it within himself to become the man that everyone's saying he's going to be, and you're not sure at the end if he is going to do it, but you definitely sense that he will."

Braga concludes: "This movie is about Picard's quest for vengeance as much as anything else, and his relationship with the Lily character, a woman from the time of war, the twenty-first century, who is, ironically, the only one who can sense in him this bloodlust." ∎

With the script well on the way, it came time to assign a director. In January of 1996, actor Jonathan Frakes, having already distinguished himself as a director in three *Star Trek* series, was appointed to the task. "The powers that be thought they should stay with someone who knew *Star Trek*, and I certainly fell into that category," explains Frakes. "All of us who have done a lot of the episodes threw our hats into the ring, and I feel fortunate to be the one that was chosen." Lobbying enthusiastically for Frakes were fellow cast members Patrick Stewart and Brent Spiner. "I certainly think their support didn't hurt," laughs Frakes. "Rick Berman is the one who I thank. He's been a champion for years. He's the one who gave me an opportunity to direct for the first time. He's been very loyal."

Stewart says that having Frakes at the helm is so perfect an idea, he doesn't understand why it took so long to become a reality: "This is proving to be as good an experience as I hoped it would be. I am most pleased that Jonathan earned the job and that he has so heartily embraced the task. He is bringing everything he learned while he was acting in and directing episodes of *Star Trek: The Next Generation* to *Star Trek: First Contact*, and it is paying off for us and for Jonathan. One can see that, given the scale of

this movie, a director, and a first-time director at that, might have been overwhelmed by it all. On the contrary, Jonathan stands so tall while he's directing, literally and figuratively. I heard a visitor on the set say, 'This is amazing. I have never seen the director of a movie this complicated appear to be as relaxed and at ease as Jonathan is.' He's really doing a wonderful job of it. It's thrilling to be here for what I think is going to be a very grand directing career for Jonathan."

As director, Frakes had a degree of input into the evolution of the final draft of the screenplay. "I certainly didn't change the structure of the script, because what we started with is something quite wonderful," he says. "Some things changed as a result of locations that I scouted, and I made some suggestions for writing scenes to location. I went to the missile silo in Arizona where we shot a big sequence of the film. They had written that it would be a missile silo, but this particular location was an actual ICBM missile in its bunker, a tube 100 feet down. Its location lent itself to a certain movement that was not indicated by the script, and there were some opportunities for stunts that I thought would be fascinating. I suggested them to the writers. They put them in, and they're a wonderful part of the film."

For inspiration prior to filming, Frakes studied

the work of several genre masters, viewing such great films as *Alien*, *Aliens*, *Close Encounters of the Third Kind*, *Blade Runner* and *Jaws*. "I looked at all the good ones," he says. "I was always told, 'Steal from the good ones if you can.' I think those are the films that audiences loved, because they combined action with storytelling, and that's what I'm hoping we did with this one." Of all the films, *Jaws* seems the most interesting choice, having little to do with invading aliens or outer space. Frakes says he selected that film because "the implied threat of the shark is what I'm hoping we do with the Borg. There's an implied threat before we actually see them. I thought the way Spielberg developed that in *Jaws* was wonderful, where a lot of it is played in reactions and with sound. It was a very good jumping off point. Whenever you reveal a villain, you want to make sure that the audience and the characters are scared first, so that the build and the tension are there."

In casting, Frakes couldn't be happier with the actors that joined the regulars in *First Contact*: "We were lucky in that we got our first choice in all three leads. Alfre Woodard, who is inarguably one of the finest actors working today, plays the female lead. James Cromwell was delightful and is finally being recognised for his talent. And Alice Krige plays the villain to the hilt. She is delicious."

All of this promises to make *First Contact* an exciting film. It has been said, perhaps as a testament to a franchise which has become its own genre, that when a *Star Trek* film is released, it is compared not to other films, but to other *Star Trek* movies. According to Producer Rick Berman, "This is the best *Star Trek* movie yet. It's full of action, drama, hope for the future, and a lot of new designs and surprises for the fans." ■

2

THE CAST

The crew of the Enterprise-E go Borg-hunting, led by Captain Picard and Lieutenant Commander Data.

PATRICK STEWART

Captain Jean-Luc Picard is a true Renaissance man. Born in LaBarre, France, he is at once a brilliant captain, a born explorer, a skilled archaeologist and a consummate diplomat. In his youth, he was something of a hell-raiser. He was failed in his first attempt to enter Starfleet, and, after he was admitted, he was subject to disciplinary action at least once. After graduation, Picard picked a fight with some Nausicaans and was almost killed. To this day, he lives with the aid of an artificial heart, a result of that encounter. In late 2366, Picard was abducted by the Borg, who assimilated him and transformed him into Locutus. As Locutus, his knowledge of Starfleet tactical information allowed the Borg to destroy an armada of thirty-nine Federation ships and their crews. Although he is blameless in this event, and in fact fought hard against the Borg programming, it is a guilt that Picard carries with him always. The violation he experienced as a result of the Borg's actions is something that the captain has never fully come to terms with.

When Gene Roddenberry first saw Patrick Stewart, he was adamant that this was not the man to sit in the Captain's chair. Now, over nine years later, it's impossible to imagine anyone else seated there. "I cannot think of anything that I have done that I could be prouder of, that would go on for life, than this," says Stewart, who, after an extremely busy year spent working on other projects, is very happy to be once again reunited with the other members of *The Next Generation* ensemble.

While Stewart felt that *Star Trek Generations* was an effective means of passing the torch from the original crew to *The Next Generation*, he nonetheless had his reservations about the film, which he thought was too dark and portrayed his character as too brooding. However, he is full of enthusiasm for *First Contact*: "We have a wonderful story, a different kind of story from *Generations*. It's a great adventure. It uses most of the principal characters effectively. It's actually quite dark at times, and that is necessarily so, it being a story that features the Borg. I feel especially pleased with it in terms of what we do with Picard this time. In *First Contact*, despite the Borg connection, we see him being very much the captain. We see him on the *Enterprise*, on the bridge and in command, which is where he should be and what he should be doing."

Stewart says that there are some rather subtle differences in the way Picard is played this time around: "Jonathan has already said, 'Picard is a little different. There are things about him that we didn't see before,' which rather pleases me. One or two

"He is a brilliant captain, a born explorer, a skilled archaeologist and a consummate diplomat."

things are deliberate and conscious, but I've a feeling that the other things are the result of the work that I've been doing in the past two years between *Star Trek Generations* and this movie. Things affect you, and you change. So he is changing. He's growing a little different. I just hope that he's as loveable and adorable as he always was." Not the least of the changes evident in the new Picard are the subtle differences in his English accent: "I had just finished making a movie, the second movie in which I play an American role, and because I was not happy with my accent in the first one, I decided that this time I would live my life sounding like an American. For three months, I was living with nothing but American sounds in my mouth. These became so much second nature that I have a feeling it's going to be that way for life, which is fine by me. So if you find that the good captain is sounding a bit more mid-Atlantic, you must not be too dismayed."

First Contact also features a Picard who is somewhat more athletic-looking than the last time we saw him: "I have been, as they say, working out, and to my surprise, I've actually been enjoying it a great deal. During the four months that I was in New York with *The Tempest*, I was preparing for this movie that I've just finished, in which I have to appear often with few clothes on, and on occasion with no clothes on. As I was supposed to play somebody that was kind of tough, I spent twelve weeks in New York working out with the most wonderful trainer. After only about three weeks, I looked in a mirror and didn't quite know who the person was looking back at me."

As for the character of Lily Sloane, Stewart feels that a "definite attraction and appeal" grows out of the experiences they share. It was Stewart who suggested a black woman for the role, and he has no time for viewers who exhibit an intolerance for this mixed pair. Racism has no place in the twentieth century, let alone the twenty-fourth. "It is a reality, I guess," he grudgingly agrees, "but it is not a part of my universe. This was one of my reasons, from the beginning, for suggesting a black actress for Lily. It's absolutely at the heart of what *Star Trek* is all about.

I don't see it as an issue. I see in Lily a tremendously attractive, intelligent woman being played by a tremendously attractive, intelligent woman and a brilliant actress."

Stewart insists the persistent rumours that he is no longer interested in the character are unfounded. He says he has made a pact with himself to take to heart the words of Captain Kirk spoken in *Star Trek Generations*, that he should never leave the captain's chair: "I have always said I would not mind coming back to *Star Trek* and to Picard as long as I had the opportunity to do other things. I still feel that way."

As to those "other things", Stewart has quite a list of credits, having appeared in such films as *Jeffrey*, *Gunmen*, *Robin Hood: Men in Tights*, *LA Story*, *Lady Jane*, *Dune*, *Excalibur* and *Hedda*. He also lent his unmistakable voice to the animated/live action feature *The Pagemaster*. Recently, Stewart completed production on the psychological thriller *Safe House*, and a comedy, *Smart Alec*. The actor took to the stage in the summer of 1995, with a production of Shakespeare's *The Tempest*. Beginning as part of New York's famed Central Park Shakespeare Festival, the production was so popular that it transferred to Broadway for a sold-out run of several months, being the first show in eighteen years to have transferred from the Park. On television, Stewart appeared in TNT's *In Search of Dr. Seuss* and played the title role in a contemporary adaptation of

Oscar Wilde's *The Canterville Ghost* for ABC and Hallmark Hall of Fame. His voice can be heard in an episode of *The Simpsons* and he has hosted several documentary series, including *The Shape of the World* and *MGM: When the Lion Roars*. As Captain Picard, Stewart received a Best Dramatic Actor nomination from the Emmys (the American TV awards) and a Screen Actors Guild nomination for Best Actor. His one-man adaptation of Charles Dickens' *A Christmas Carol* in the 1994-95 Broadway production earned him a Drama Desk Award for Best Solo Performer, and an Olivier Award nomination for Best Actor when the show moved to London.

All this work only serves to make him more excited about returning to take his rightful place in the coveted captain's chair in *First Contact*: "I think it's the best *Star Trek* movie story that I have yet encountered. It looks to me that it may well do what I have always pleaded for — be a wonderful movie which just happens to be *Star Trek*. I want to be the first actor in the history of the world who can continue in a successful movie franchise like *Star Trek*, making every movie better and better than the one before it, and at the same time fill my working life in between with other movies, with theatre work, with whatever I want to do. It's very, very important to me that our movies be the best movies that we can make and that we go on making them. And that, I guess, is that." ■

JONATHAN FRAKES

William T. Riker is the first officer of the *U.S.S. Enterprise*. A distinguished Starfleet commander, Riker has been decorated five times. An unconventional, headstrong leader, as well as consummate lady's man, Riker was born in Valdez, Alaska in 2335 and graduated from Starfleet Academy in 2357, ranking eighth in his class. Riker got the choice assignment of first officer of the *Enterprise*-D because of actions he took on the *Starship Hood*. It was that action, in which he refused to let his captain beam into a dangerous situation, that convinced Captain Jean-Luc Picard that Riker should be his Number One. Although William Riker has been offered his own command more than once, he prefers to remain on the *Enterprise* under the command of Captain Picard, an experience he finds worth the delay in his own career. The commander has also been known to play a mean jazz trombone.

For Jonathan Frakes, directing as well as starring in *Star Trek: First Contact* is a dream come true. The actor-turned-director contends that the task "has been the most challenging job that I have ever had to undertake." While portraying Picard's Number One is the role of a lifetime, Frakes is grateful that *Star Trek* has afforded him the opportunity to wear more than just one hat.

In *Star Trek: The Next Generation*'s third season, Frakes became the first actor from that series to move to the other side of the camera, taking the helm for the episode "The Offspring". "The first time, it was a tough push to get Rick Berman to commit to doing it," laughs Frakes. "I had to spend about 300 hours in the editing room, and I followed all the other directors around. It was an interesting education at 'Paramount University'. I can see that subsequently, they have been more comfortable letting actors behind the camera."

Frakes followed this with other directing assignments, including more episodes of *The Next Generation*, as well as *Star Trek: Deep Space Nine* and *Star Trek: Voyager*. All this prepared him for what Frakes terms "the most exciting job of my career so far." He credits Producer Rick Berman, who gave him his first opportunity, for this chance of a lifetime as well. According to Frakes, *First Contact* is a wonderful action film combined with top notch storytelling. "There are a number of themes," he says. "One of the dominant themes is friendship. It's the Data/Picard friendship that is explored. Another theme is the idea of someone from our time, or sixty years from now, the twenty-first century, landing in the twenty-fourth century. Alfre's character, Lily Sloane, ends up on the *Enterprise*, so the audience gets a chance to see the twenty-fourth century through her eyes. The third theme is this reluctant hero Zefram Cochrane, played by James Cromwell. He develops warp drive and thus *Star Trek* is born. The character is an alcoholic, a ne'er-do-well, and yet he's also a brilliant scientist and inventor. I think the reluctant hero is quite an interesting character."

As if the incredible pressure of directing his first feature film wasn't enough, Frakes had the added responsibility of directing himself: "It's always more challenging on the days that you have to work as an actor and a director. First of all, between hair, make-up and wardrobe, it's another part of your day spent preparing that way. You have to trust outside sources. In many cases, I used some of my peers whose taste and judgement I trust, Brent and Patrick and LeVar and Matthew Leonetti, the DP [director of photography], so that I have another set of eyes on my performance in addition to worrying about the

"A distinguished Starfleet commander, an unconventional, headstrong leader and a consummate lady's man."

composition of the shots and the movement of the camera and the storytelling. It's challenging, but it was also rewarding."

As for the cast reuniting on this movie, Frakes says it was "a delight. It's become a cliché, but we really are a family. It was fun to have a reunion and around that reunion to make a movie. Patrick, for one, has never been better than he is in this film. Brent has never been better. This is a credit both to them as actors and to the story. Some of the best work in the film is done by Patrick and Alfre and their scenes together." In fact, Frakes cites the sequences between Patrick Stewart and Alfre Woodard as the most personally rewarding aspect of directing *First Contact*: "The few days that we spent doing the pivotal acting scene between Alfre and Patrick — it was just a pleasure to be on the set to watch these artists work."

"I'm looking forward to the finished project," says Frakes, "and I'm looking forward to my next job." Since *First Contact* will launch him well on the way to a successful career as a multi-million dollar feature film director, will he still want to return to play Commander Riker? "I would certainly be proud to play Riker as long as they will have me," he says. "My involvement with *Star Trek* has given me opportunities

"William Riker has been offered his own command more than once, but prefers to remain on the Enterprise *under Captain Jean-Luc Picard."*

I never thought I would have. I'm extremely grateful."

Jonathan Frakes has appeared in such television series as *Falcon Crest*, *Paper Dolls*, *Hill Street Blues*, *Bare Essence* and *The Doctors*, where he worked with Terry Farrell. He won critical acclaim for his performances in the mini-series *Dream West* and *North and South*, and recently starred in the ABC movie-of-the-week *Brothers of the Frontier*. Frakes hosted UPN's *Paranormal Borderline* and currently hosts the Discovery Channel's *Sights and Sounds*.

On the other side of the camera, Frakes has directed episodes of *Star Trek: The Next Generation*, *Star Trek: Deep Space Nine*, *Star Trek: Voyager*, *Diagnosis: Murder* and *University Hospital*. He also directed the CD-ROM *Star Trek: Klingon*. Born and raised in Pennsylvania, he is married to actress Genie Francis, whom he first met whilst working on the TV series *Bare Essence*. ∎

BRENT SPINER

Lieutenant Commander Data is an android built by the late Dr. Noonien Soong. While Data was created without the capacity to feel emotions, the android's neural net, his positronic brain, has been evolving constantly in an inexplicable quest to become more human. Dr. Soong's earlier android, Data's rogue 'brother' Lore, was erratic, antisocial and fully capable of experiencing emotions. It was Lore who stole the emotion chip Soong had created for Data, and only when Data was forced to deactivate Lore did the chip go to its rightful owner. Data hesitated to install the chip until the events in *Star Trek Generations*, but now he experiences the full spectrum of human feelings, albeit still with some degree of uncertainty.

"As an actor, I *have* to do other things," says Brent Spiner, the actor under Data's gold make-up, "I have to keep challenging myself, but it's interesting now that we're into the features to come back and play Data every couple of years. I like seeing everyone in this cast again, and I'm quite comfortable playing Data again in *Star Trek: First Contact*. I know the character pretty well by now and, if I don't, well, we've got a real problem!

"Data has evolved a step at a time," says Spiner, "and the emotion chip is another step in that evolution, another colour in the palette. I'm sure there may be other colours to play in the future, if we do more films, but I don't worry about it, really. I leave that to the writers. They've always been very good about coming up with creative things for Data to do and interesting developments that make him more human. That makes him more interesting for me to play. I've had that rare chance to create a dramatic character over a long period of time. It's been what, almost a decade? It's been a really great experience,

and I'm very thankful I got to be Data."

Born in Houston, Texas, Brent Spiner made his motion picture starring début in *Star Trek Generations* after appearing in Woody Allen's *Stardust Memories* and playing a cameo role in *Miss Firecracker*. He has guest-starred in such television series as *The Outer Limits*, *Deadly Game*, *Cheers*, *The Twilight Zone*, *Night Court* and *Hill Street Blues*, and appeared in the TV films *Pie in the Sky* and *Kingfish*. Recently, Spiner featured in the movie *Phenomenon* with John Travolta, and played Dr. Okun in the blockbuster *Independence Day*. He also co-stars alongside Jack Lemmon and Walter Matthau in the upcoming *Out to Sea*.

During his fourth season hiatus from *Star Trek: The Next Generation*, the multi-talented Spiner co-produced and released a music album: *Ol' Yellow Eyes is Back*. Some of the background vocals were provided by 'The Sunspots', who were none other than Patrick Stewart, Jonathan Frakes, LeVar Burton and Michael Dorn. ■

"Data now experiences the full spectrum of human feelings, albeit still with some degree of uncertainty."

LEVAR BURTON

Lieutenant **Commander Geordi La Forge** began his tour of duty on the *U.S.S. Enterprise* as a lieutenant, junior grade, in the position of flight controller. Within one year had been promoted to full lieutenant and chief engineer. La Forge was born blind, but, during the era covered in *Star Trek: The Next Generation* and *Star Trek Generations*, was able to see through the use of a VISOR (Visual Instrument and Sensory Organ Replacement). The device transmitted visual data to La Forge on a wider spectrum than human eyes. *Star Trek: First Contact* marks the first appearance of his new artificial eyes, an improvement over the cumbersome VISOR. La Forge is an expert on the technology that runs the *Enterprise*, but to date has not been as adept at forging relationships with women. His best friend is the android Data.

"It was great to be able to see everybody again," says LeVar Burton of his experience on *First Contact*, "and to work together. There was actually only one or two days during the schedule where we were all together. Those were the best days, as far as I was concerned, because, and I know I'm not the first one to say this, the greatest part of the experience of doing *The Next Generation* was coming to work every day and laughing with my friends. That's the part that I miss the most about not doing the show. I miss the fun with my friends. Those few days on *First Contact* when we were all together was like being home." Burton was also pleased with the film's choice of director. "It was great to be able to support my friend Jonathan Frakes as a director," he says, adding that Frakes' performance in this capacity was "awesome. He did a great job." As to his own assessment of the film, Burton laughs, "I was less tired this time, because I hadn't done a full calendar year of

The Next Generation."

La Forge's new VISORless look is something Burton has looked forward to for a long time. The actor sums up his feelings about losing the cumbersome and uncomfortable prop in "one word: hallelujah!" But weren't the new contact lenses used to achieve the look of La Forge's artificial eyes uncomfortable as well? "Not nearly as uncomfortable as the VISOR," he states.

LeVar Burton received an Emmy award for his performance as Kunta Kinte in the television miniseries *Roots* and has appeared in such films as *The Hunter* and *Looking for Mr. Goodbar*. He is the host and co-executive prod-ucer of the PBS children's television series *Reading Rainbow*, now in its thirteenth season. An accomplished director, Burton has helmed episodes of both *Star Trek: Voyager* and *Star Trek: Deep Space Nine*. His company, Eagle Nation Films, has just signed an exclusive deal with Paramount Pictures to produce television and feature films. Burton is currently putting the finishing touches to his first novel. ■

"Star Trek: First Contact *marks the first appearance of La Forge's new artificial eyes*"

MICHAEL DORN

Worf, son of Mogh, is the first Klingon ever to serve in Starfleet. He was born on the Klingon homeworld, but orphaned when his parents were killed in a Romulan attack on the Khitomer outpost. The young Worf was rescued by Sergey Rozhenko, who, along with his wife Helena, raised the Klingon child as his own. On the *Enterprise*-D, Worf served as chief of security.

Discovering that he had a younger brother named Kurn who still lived, Worf returned with him to the homeworld to uncover the traitor who betrayed Khitomer to the Romulans. When it was found that the House of Duras was at fault, Worf accepted discommendation rather than cast the Klingon Empire into civil war. When civil war broke out in late 2367, Worf regained his honour by supporting the regime of Gowron. Worf currently serves as strategic operations officer of Deep Space 9, where he is often in charge of the *U.S.S. Defiant*. In opposing the Klingon attack on Cardassia, Gowron, head of the Klingon High Council, again stripped him of his standing in the Empire. Worf has one son, Alexander (by the late half-human, half-Klingon ambassador K'Ehleyr), who is currently living with the Rozhenkos.

Star Trek: First Contact marks Michael Dorn's third appearance in a *Star Trek* feature film. In *Star Trek VI: The Undiscovered Country*, Dorn appeared in a cameo role, playing Lieutenant Commander Worf's own grandfather. Now, in the middle of his second year as Worf on *Star Trek: Deep Space Nine*, Dorn returns to his *Star Trek: The Next Generation* crewmates for their second outing on the big screen. "Worf's role in *First Contact* is basically something he was cut out for," explains Dorn. "He is just out there, in a dangerous situation, and he's fighting his tail off. He's beating the hell out of the Borg. Worf comes over from Deep Space 9 in the *Defiant*. He's in the middle of a battle, and they beam him over to the *Enterprise* just before he can destroy himself and the ship. Plus, there are moments where he gets into head-to-head confrontations with Captain Picard. That's good. It shows the characters in a different light than we've seen them in before. I'm very happy with what I got to do in the movie. Jonathan did a great job directing it, and I think people are really going to like it."

Dorn has been portraying the gruff but popular Klingon for almost a decade, a statistic he is quick to remark on: "It makes me feel old, honoured, surprised. It's unbelievable to be working on one thing for ten years, to play one character for ten years. That's rare. To be in make-up for ten years, that's something I never thought I would be able to survive. But I have, and here I am."

Michael Dorn was born in Luling, Texas and raised in Pasadena, California. His film appearances include *Timemaster*, *Jagged Edge*, *Rocky* and *The Demon Seed*. On television he was a regular cast member for three years in the series *CHiPS*, and played recurring roles in *Days of Our Lives* and *Capitol*. Dorn starred in the Showtime feature *Amanda and the Alien*, and guest-starred in the series *The Outer Limits*, *Getting By*, *Hotel*, *Knot's Landing* and *Falcon Crest*. He is the host of *The World of Wonder* for the Discovery Channel. Dorn recently starred in the CD-ROM *Mission Critical*, which won the *CD-ROM Advisor*'s Golden Trial Award as the best game of the year. Currently, Dorn continues his role as Lieutenant Commander Worf on *Star Trek: Deep Space Nine*. When not acting, he enjoys piloting his own F-86 jet plane. ∎

"Worf was born on the Klingon homeworld, but orphaned when his parents were killed in a Romulan attack."

GATES McFADDEN

Dr. Beverly Crusher is the chief medical officer onboard the *Enterprise*-E. One of Starfleet's top physicians, her tenure on the *Enterprise*-D was actually interrupted when she left to take up a temporary post as head of Starfleet Medical, returning after a year. Dedicated to her job, she is often the voice of reason: to her, the medical oath means more than just words. She is the widow of Lieutenant Commander Jack Crusher, who was one of Captain Picard's close friends. Crusher has one son, Wesley, who also served aboard the *Enterprise* for a time.

Coming two years after *Star Trek Generations*, Gates McFadden says that the reality of the new film didn't sink in until the entire cast assembled to shoot a scene set onboard the newly designed *Enterprise*-E: "I think the scene in the observation lounge was when it really hit me. Even though it was a new observation lounge on a new *Enterprise*, it still hit home that, 'Yes, we *are* really back and, yes, we really are doing it again.'"

Though her role in *Star Trek: First Contact* is not as large as some fans would prefer, she is an indisputable part of the *Enterprise* crew. No *Star Trek: The Next Generation* film would be complete without Dr. Crusher: "I don't really have a substantial amount to do in the film. I'm sort of doing a bit here and a bit there in some scenes, but there are some scenes with almost all of us together on the bridge. Those were exciting." Recalling the shoot, McFadden sums it up by saying, "We were laughing a lot. I had fun, and I'd have to say I like the idea of getting together every couple of years to do a movie."

McFadden is extremely busy with other projects and opportunities, including an invitation to return to teaching, and the actress isn't concerned about being identified with this role in particular. "To tell you the truth," says McFadden, "it's the kids' reaction that gives me the greatest pleasure about doing *Star Trek*. It's wonderful that it is so imaginative and creative. I'm glad to be a part of it. I get many kids telling me they would like a mom like Beverly, and they feel I can solve their problems. It's not an easy world to grow up in. It's tough. It's nice to think we are doing our bit to help."

Born and raised in Ohio, Gates McFadden graduated with a BA from Brandeis University. She studied improvisation and mime with Jacques LeCoq in Paris, before moving to New York to embark on her acting career. She has since taught acting at New York University Graduate School of the Arts, the University of Pittsburgh and Brandeis University. Among her film credits are *Star Trek Generations*, *Taking Care of Business*, *The Hunt for Red October* and *The Muppets Take Manhattan*. Her television work includes recurring roles on *Mad About You* and *Marker*, and guest-starring appearances in *Dream On*, *Party of Five*, *The Cosby Show*, *Mystery Dance*, *Wizard of Elm Street* and *True Confessions*.

A professional choreographer, McFadden served as director of choreography and puppet movement on Jim Henson's feature, *Labyrinth*, as well as assisting on the fantasy sequences in *Dreamchild*. *Star Trek* fans might also remember Dr. Crusher teaching a certain android to dance in *The Next Generation* episode "Data's Day". On the stage, she appeared alongside several of her fellow *Star Trek: The Next Generation* cast members in a production of Tom Stoppard's play *Every Good Boy Deserves Favour*. McFadden says her favourite *Star Trek: The Next Generation* experience was her stint in the director's chair for the seventh season episode "Genesis". ∎

"Dedicated to her job, she is often the voice of reason: to her, the medical oath means more than just words."

MARINA SIRTIS

Deanna Troi is the *U.S.S. Enterprise*'s half-human, half-Betazoid counselor, a strong empath with the ability to read emotions. Prior to joining Starfleet, she studied psychology at the University of Betazed, where she became romantically involved with William Riker. When the two found themselves serving together on board the *Enterprise*-D, they mutually agreed to put their former feelings for each other aside, though they remain close friends. Her mother, the formidable Lwaxana Troi, has been a frequent visitor to the *Enterprise*, often much to her daughter's chagrin.

"Sometimes, I'm more Troi than me when we're filming," says actress Marina Sirtis, speaking of her *Star Trek* alter ego. In person, the outspoken, outgoing and definitely British-sounding Sirtis seems as different as day and night from the more subdued, introspective *Enterprise* counselor. "Troi has been a calming influence on me," she contends. "I've become more patient, more understanding since I started playing her. But I want to bring more of Marina's vitality to Deanna, too."

Prior to being cast in the role of the ship's counselor, Sirtis actually auditioned for the role of the security chief, Tasha Yar. Troi came into her own in the last years of the programme, particularly in the final two seasons, when Jeri Taylor (now executive producer of *Star Trek: Voyager*) made refining the Troi character her personal quest. In this period, we saw Troi as a Romulan impersonator, a rifle-toting Western gunslinger and a Klingon love interest. Each new facet to her character left the audience wanting more.

Sirtis is up front about her feelings that *Star Trek: The Next Generation* was cancelled before its time. She felt there was still several years' worth of interesting exploration to be done, both in outer space and within the character of the counselor. "To be honest," she says, "I'd rather come back more than every couple of years. We all miss the series and we've all kept in touch. I was talking with Terry Farrell [of *Star Trek: Deep Space Nine*], who's a very good friend of mine. She said, 'You really miss being here, don't you?' and I said, 'Yeah, I really do.' So, the thought of getting together every couple of years is a delight."

Marina Sirtis was born in London to Greek parents. She graduated from the Guild Hall School of Music and Drama, then joined the Worthing Repertory Theatre. Her films include *Death Wish 3*, *Blind Date* and *The Thief of Baghdad*. Before joining the cast of *Star Trek: The Next Generation*, Sirtis appeared on television in Britain in such series as *Sherlock Holmes*, *Minder* and *Hazel* and starred in the British television film *The Last Chance*. After *The Next Generation* left the air, she appeared on television in *Robin's Hoods*. Recently, Marina made her critically acclaimed American theatrical début in Hartford Stage's production of *Loot*. ∎

"Troi is the U.S.S. Enterprise's half-human, half-Betazoid counselor, an empath with the ability to read emotions."

ALFRE WOODARD

Lily Sloane is a headstrong twenty-first century survivor of World War Three. As Zefram Cochrane's assistant, she is caught up in the struggle for the future and is swept into Captain Picard's battle with the Borg on the *Starship Enterprise*. As a product of a post-apocalyptic world, she alone recognises the turbulent emotions driving Picard and forces the captain to confront his inner demons.

"It was a great experience for me," says Alfre Woodard, who portrays Lily Sloane. "I've always chosen things that interest me or excite me. That's what I've done my entire career, really." Woodard says that her excitement began the moment she read the script for *Star Trek: First Contact*: "As I read it, I was totally on edge. I was seeing it in my head. It was to the point where I was talking out loud, pulling for some of the characters or gasping at what some of the other characters were doing. When I got to the set, it was a joy as well. I loved working with Jonathan Frakes and with Patrick Stewart. I'm glad I did the film."

Fighting the Borg can be a pretty harrowing experience, and Woodard didn't shirk from it. "I had to run all over the place and get pretty dirty," she laughs. "I got a few bumps and bruises, but that was okay, because I wanted it to look real. I did as many stunts as I could, because I didn't want to be a weenie. I didn't like the idea of a stuntwoman doing the hard stuff, and then me just popping in there, looking all sweaty but having done nothing."

Alfre Woodard is an accomplished actress with quite a few awards and nominations to her credit. She received an Academy Award nomination for *Cross Creek*, and earned a Best Actress award from the Screen Actors Guild and an Emmy nomination for her starring performance in the Hallmark Hall of Fame production of *The Piano Lesson*. Woodard also earned two Emmy Awards for a guest-starring role on *Hill Street Blues* and for the pilot episode of *LA Law*. Her television credits include Emmy Award-nominated performances in *St. Elsewhere*, the PBS production *Words by Heart* and the TV films *A Mother's Courage: The Mary Thomas Story* and John Sayles' *Unnatural Causes*. In addition, Woodard was honoured with an ACE award for her portrayal of Winnie Mandela in the HBO presentation *Mandela*. Her films include *Crooklyn*, *Bopha!*, *Passion Fish*, *Rich in Love*, *Blue Chips*, *Heart and Souls*, *Grand Canyon*, *The Gun in Betty Lou's Handbag*, *Scrooged*, *Miss Firecracker*, *H.E.A.L.T.H.*, *Remember My Name*, and the recent *How to Make an American Quilt* and *Primal Fear*. ∎

JAMES CROMWELL

Zefram Cochrane is the human scientist who developed the warp drive, which allows starships to travel at velocities in excess of the speed of light, breaching the incredible distances between the stars. When Cochrane created the first warp ship, he ushered in the very beginnings of humanity's 'star trek'. As one of the twenty-fourth century's greatest legends, he is a figure of unparalleled renown. Universities, cities and even whole worlds are named in his honour. But history preserves the myth without knowing the man, as the crew of the *Enterprise*-E find out, and the Zefram Cochrane of the twenty-first century is quite different from the Cochrane they expect. The character of Zefram Cochrane first appeared in the 1967 *Star Trek* episode, "Metamorphosis", and was portrayed by actor Glenn Corbett.

Acclaimed actor James Cromwell plays Cochrane in *Star Trek: First Contact*. "Instead of having to play a legend," he explains, "what I had to play was someone who was reluctant to become a legend. That's eminently playable. He had a very strong reaction, which was that it frightened, confused, confounded and disturbed him."

Star Trek, more than any other science fiction series, has always been closely identified with America's space effort. Cromwell finds significance in portraying the man solely responsible for taking humanity to the stars, just as possible evidence of life on Mars was being discovered: "I was profoundly excited and moved at this point in time to play Zefram Cochrane, and what he represents, in this fictional story about man's aspirations and his future. I'm a firm believer that contact has already been made and has been suppressed by the United States Government. I believe that all the films about contact represent the strivings of humanity to begin to tell the truth and to recognise and accept our rightful place in the universe. That I get an opportunity to represent the man who has the courage to reach his hand out and embrace the Other, regardless of the consequences because that's his destiny, is a real privilege."

James Cromwell recently earned an Academy Award nomination for Best Supporting Actor for his portrayal of Farmer Hoggett in the film *Babe*. His numerous film credits include *The People vs. Larry Flynt*, *Eraser*, three of the *Revenge of the Nerds* films, *Pink Cadillac*, *The Man with Two Brains* and *The Cheap Detective*. His first film was Neil Simon's *Murder by Death*. No stranger to Roddenberry's universe, Cromwell has appeared twice on *Star Trek: The Next Generation* and also in *Star Trek: Deep Space Nine*, though it is not always easy to recognise him — he was buried under elaborate alien make-ups in two of the roles. He also portrayed Stretch Cunningham on *All in the Family*, and has had guest roles in *Strange Luck*, *The Client*, *Picket Fences*, *LA Law*, *Home Improvement*, *Hill Street Blues*, *Dallas*, *M*A*S*H* and *The Twilight Zone*. ∎

ALICE KRIGE

The Borg: a race of cybernetic organisms who possess a collective mentality, the Borg are bent on assimilating all other life forms. Each new encounter brings startling revelations about these nigh-invincible opponents. But the biggest and most surprising secret about the Borg Collective is revealed in *Star Trek: First Contact*: the Collective has a Queen. Not precisely an individual in her own right, she is a nexus for the hive mind; an entity, a hungry presence, a personality given body that simply *is* the Collective. Stepping into the daunting task of embodying an entire race is Alice Krige.

Krige says she was both "delighted" and "apprehensive" when she was given the role. "I always have my heart in my mouth when I start something new," says the actress, "so that was par for the course. You never know whether or not you're going to make the role work. There's a very extraordinary and unusual use of language in *Star Trek*. It has a quality and rhythm all it's own. It's not written like colloquial speech. I found that particularly interesting, but I didn't necessarily think that it was going to be easy to pull that off. So I guess that it was with a mix of exhilaration and trepidation that I took the part."

But how does one portray an alien that isn't even a single presence, but a sort of hub for the mind of a whole species? Krige claims, "She says 'I am the Collective.' She's it. The Borg population simply exists as an aspect or a function of her. She *is* the Collective. She's the imagination. She's the mind. The Borg we've met so far have just been her tentacles, not even her drones but her instruments. Let me tell you, not one person I spoke to had the same take on who she was."

Despite the gruelling hours, Krige loved her time working on *First Contact*: "It really is enjoyable to play that kind of bad guy, and I really, really love the people that I worked with."

Alice Krige studied Psychology and Drama at Rhodes University, South Africa, and then proceeded to receive a Diploma in acting from London's Central School of Speech and Drama. She has appeared in such films as *Cinergi*, *Habitat*, *Institute Benjamenta*, *Sleepwalkers*, *Haunted Summer*, *Barfly*, *See You in the Morning*, *King David*, *Ghost Story*, and *Chariots of Fire*. Her American television work includes *Donor Unknown*, *Joseph*, *Jack Reed: An Honest Cop*, *Deliver Them from Evil*, *Ladykillers* and *Dream West*, in which she appeared alongside Jonathan Frakes. Alice Krige has also appeared in *Sharpe's Honour*, *Devil's Advocate* and *The Red and the Black* on British television. ∎

"She is an entity, a hungry presence, a personality given body that simply is the Collective."

DWIGHT SCHULTZ

Lieutenant Reginald Barclay was one of the most popular recurring characters in *Star Trek: The Next Generation*. The Starfleet systems diagnostic engineer transferred to the *Enterprise*-D in 2366. Geordi La Forge found that while Barclay was an extremely skilled engineer, he was a social recluse. Barclay preferred to live out fantasies in the holodeck, rather than form bonds with real people. La Forge and Troi helped him overcome some of these tendencies, though Barclay still remains a somewhat nervous personality.

"Barclay wasn't even in it originally," explains Dwight Schultz, speaking of his cameo appearance

in the film. "It was Jonathan Frakes' idea." When *The Next Generation* franchise moved to the big screen, Schultz thought he'd played the highly strung, anxiety ridden Reg Barclay for the last time. That might have been the case, except for a clever connection made by Director Frakes. The script for *Star Trek: First Contact* called for Zefram Cochrane to be accosted by an over-zealous fan, a lieutenant who would shower Cochrane with embarrassing compliments like an all too enthusiastic puppy dog: "It was Jonathan Frakes' idea to bring me into it, because I was a lieutenant that everyone who had seen *The Next Generation* was familiar with. Jonathan called me and said, 'It's just a little cameo. Would you do it?' I said, 'Of course, I'd love to be in the movie. I'd give anything to be in it.'"

Once the actor's availability was confirmed, the writers set about a quick rewrite to make the anonymous lieutenant more in keeping with the inimitable Barclay: "They made it Barclay-esque, more recognisable, as opposed to just a generic 'Hello. How are you? It's nice to meet you,' which was what the character was originally." The results make the interaction between Cochrane and Barclay a special moment for *Star Trek* fans: "It's like a groupie following a famous actor around. He ambushes Jamie Cromwell and just goes on and on. Those who are familiar with *The Next Generation* and Barclay will get a kick out of his enthusiasm. It was only one day of shooting, but it was a blast. I love Jonathan. He's so much fun to be with. I'm very appreciative that he brought me in."

Barclay began life when Schultz was invited to guest star in the third season *Star Trek: The Next Generation* episode, "Hollow Pursuits". That one appearance turned into one episode a season for four seasons and a spot on *Star Trek: Voyager*. Schultz's film work includes *The Fan*, *The Temp*, *Fat Man and Little Boy* and *The Long Walk Home*. On television, he has appeared in *Touched By an Angel*, *Nowhere Man*, *Hart to Hart*, *Deadly Games*, *The Outer Limits*, and numerous other programmes. While these days Schultz claims he is most identified with the *Star Trek* lieutenant, the actor will never be forgotten as Howling Mad Murdock in the series *The A-Team*. ■

ROBERT PICARDO

On *Star Trek: Voyager*, he's the Emergency Medical Hologram, a character without a name. Robert Picardo plays 'the doctor', a holographic program created for use in emergency situations when a ship's physician is unavailable. The EMH, as it is called, is a combination of artificial intelligence and controlled forcebeams, programmed with a complete medical database. When the *Voyager* was lost in deep space and its chief medical officer killed, the EMH was activated and forced to take over permanent medical duties. On that series, the EMH is in constant operation and has, over three years, developed a kind of consciousness of its own. But as computer software, there isn't any reason that other EMH programs couldn't exist elsewhere, a fact which allows Robert Picardo to make a brief but very funny cameo in *Star Trek: First Contact*.

"The thing started as kind of a tongue-in-cheek joke to Rick Berman, and then clearly got out of hand," says Picardo. "I was chatting with Rick in his office and I said, 'I have a question Rick. If an Emergency Medical Hologram is a new technology in Starfleet and we have one on the *Voyager*, and they are building a brand new *Enterprise*, wouldn't the new ship have an EMH program? It would be standard equipment.' And he smiled, and I said, 'Look, I'm not trying to pad my part here in the franchise. I'm just watching out for your logic, Mr. Berman,' and he smiled again."

That might have been the end of it, but Picardo kept on with his suggestion: "Jonathan Frakes directed an episode of *Voyager* called "Projections", which featured my character, so we got to be pals. When I learned that Jonathan was going to direct the movie, I mentioned the idea to him, and he thought it was a funny idea. I guess Brannon [Braga] and Ron Moore decided to give it a try. My character being software, there could be an infinite number of EMH programs, and they don't all necessarily have to look alike. My personal wish is that some of them look like Claudia Schiffer, but let's face it, I look the way I look, and if it's the same program then in theory I could be aboard all Starfleet vessels at this point."

Although the software is technically the same, the version of the EMH activated on the *Enterprise* is not exactly like the one on the *Voyager* today. This lead to a subtly different performance from the actor. "I played it very much the way I played the character in the pilot of *Star Trek: Voyager*," Picardo explains. "Because Dr. Crusher says that she hates that thing, referring to the Emergency Medical Hologram, I reasoned that I was very, very rarely used, so that my personality would be very much like my newly activated personality on *Voyager*." Picardo chuckles and adds, "So I am not nearly as colourful and sexy as I am on *Voyager*."

Born in Philadelphia, Pennsylvania, Robert Picardo is a veteran of television, theatre and film. On television, he starred in *China Beach* and *The Wonder Years*. On Broadway, he has created two leading roles, in *Tribute* (with Jack Lemmon) and *Gemini*. Picardo has appeared in two dozen feature films, including *The Howling*, *Legend*, *Explorers*, *Innerspace*, *Matinee*, *Gremlins 2* and *Revenge of the Nerds 4*. He also lent his vocal talents to *Total Recall* and *The Pagemaster*. ∎

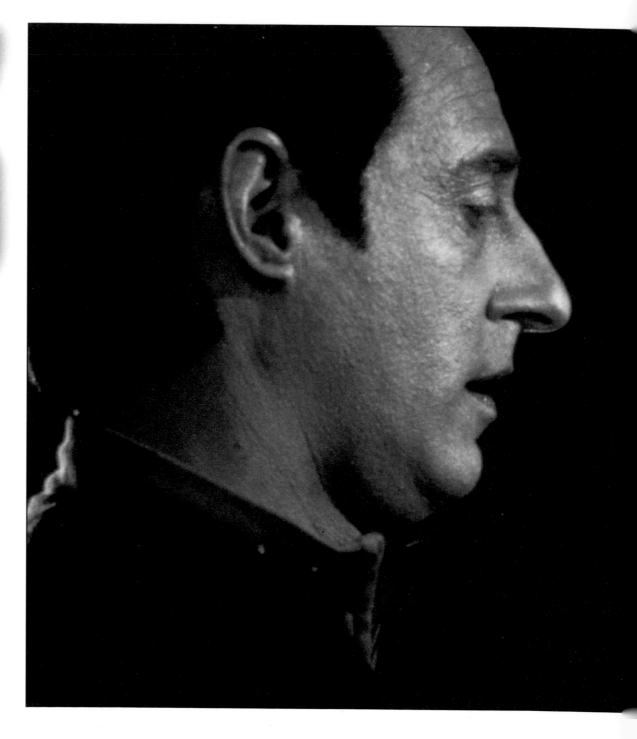

BEHIND THE SCENES

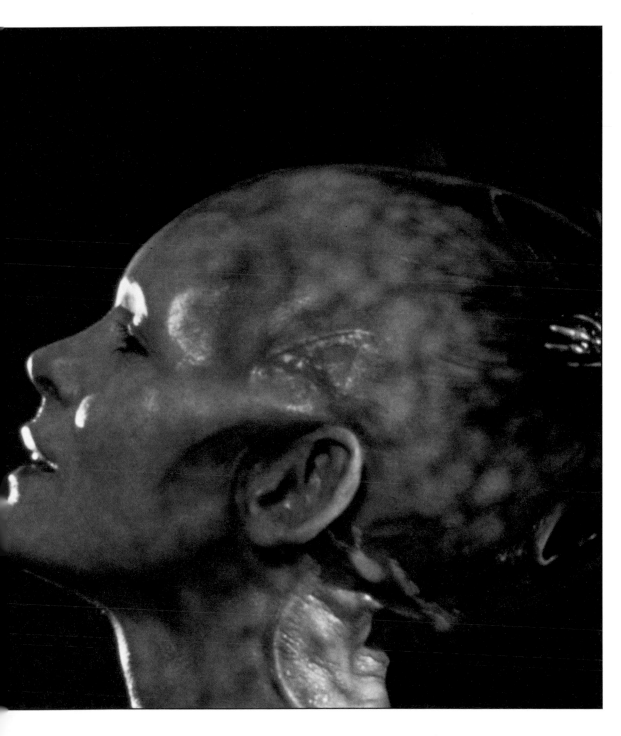

An emotional moment for Data as he comes face to face with the Collective personified — the Borg Queen.

This page: *The production design crew's work defines the film's look.*

Opposite above: *The costume design offices.*

Opposite below: *Costumes and make-up needed constant attention during filming.*

O**n any movie, a large number of creative** talents come together to help the screenwriters, producers and director realise their vision. For *Star Trek: First Contact*, the finest personnel were needed to maintain the exacting standards already set for the series.

Before filming could begin, the input of the production design and costume teams was needed. Production Designer Herman Zimmerman led the crew that determined the movie's visual 'look' as ini-

tially described by the screenwriters. The first people involved in this process are invariably the illustrators and set designers, whose role it is to come up with the initial concepts and design sketches. A team of over 100 construction workers, illustrators, set designers and model builders were then set to work creating the complex sets, props and models required for the shoot.

Also needed before the cameras roll are the film's many and varied costumes. In Costume Designer Deborah Everton, *Star Trek: First Contact* had one of the best. It was her task to dress the movie's characters in a convincing way for both the twenty-first and twenty-fourth century. Deborah was helped by a dedicated team of wardrobe personnel, dressers and assistants, who had a hand in everything from Patrick Stewart's tuxedo to an extra's shoes.

Academy-award-winning make-up artist, Michael Westmore, was given the task of creating a fiercer, more menacing Borg for the big screen. Michael comes from a respected family of make-up artists and has been involved with *Star Trek* for many years now. The make-up required for *Star Trek: First Contact* was so work intensive, he needed to supervise two make-up teams on the movie.

Once shooting commenced, a great many more people became involved. Working closely with first-time feature film director Jonathan Frakes was Director of Photography Matthew F. Leonetti. Leonetti has previously worked on such hits as *Jagged Edge*, *Poltergeist* and *Dead Again*, and was responsible for

the movie's stunning photography.

Frakes was backed up by a whole team of specialists, working on such areas as the storyboards, second unit direction, transportation and so forth. He was particularly lucky to have onboard Terry Frazzee, to handle the spectacular pyrotechnics, and Ron Rondell, who worked as Stunt Coordinator. Both are vital roles and Frazzee's and Rondell's experience ensured a trouble-free shoot.

Once principal photography was completed, it was the turn of the special visual effects masters at Industrial Light & Magic to leap into action. This company was formed by George Lucas and John Dykstra in 1975 to work on *Star Wars* and their contributions to the film industry are legendary. On this occasion, the workload was so great, they worked alongside a number of other companies, including Pacific Ocean Post, Illusion Arts, Matteworld Digital, and VisionArt Design and Animation. Their work was supervised by John Knoll and David Takemura and it is their combined technical know-how that made the impossible happen on screen.

And finally, there are the essential components of soundtrack and editing, which can make or break a movie. *Star Trek: First Contact* is lucky to have Oscar-winning Jerry Goldsmith on hand to write the score. In the editing suite was John W. Wheeler.

All these skilled artists and craftsmen, plus a small army of unsung heroes, worked together to bring *Star Trek: First Contact* to life. ■

PRODUCTION DESIGN

The latest in a distinguished line. The new Sovereign *class U.S.S. Enterprise* NCC-1701-E.

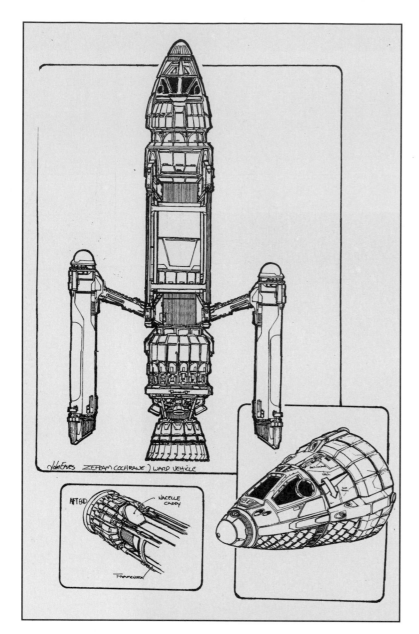

Above: *John Eaves'
design sketch for
the* Phoenix.
Right: *The Titan
II missile silo.*

S**tar Trek: First Contact's production depart-**
ment began work on 2 January 1996, with
filming scheduled to start on 8 April.
Supervising a team of over 100 workers, illustrators,
set designers and model builders was Production
Designer Herman Zimmerman. This team had but
four months to construct all the sets required,
including Zefram Cochrane's warp ship, an entirely
new *U.S.S. Enterprise*, a twenty-first century Montana
town, a 1930s nightclub and a pair of Borg ships.

Zefram Cochrane's warp ship, the *Phoenix*, was an
inspired piece of set design, inspired not only by the
script but by a deactivated Titan II Missile. "It was
one of our serious construction problems," says
Zimmerman. "If we were going to have to construct
the inside of a ballistic missile silo, we would have
spent probably over a million dollars for that one set.
That would have made a serious dent in our construction budget. As it was, it became a location, and
we put that cost in the location manager's budget.
We built a dummy cockpit, that looked like the cockpit we built for the soundstage and for the model,
and literally lifted it atop the housing for the warhead on the Titan missile in Arizona. It was quite a
logistical feat, and our construction coordinator and
his crew did a magnificent job. We literally went

Photo courtesy of Industrial Light & Magic.

down there and measured it, came back, did the drawings, built the thing, took it down, and it fitted perfectly. It was one of those things that almost never happens. But this picture was full of things like that.

"The Titan missile is 110 feet high. The capsule itself is about fourteen feet high. The diameter's ten feet. The interior is, minus some fire wall that you imagine is there, only about eight feet deep and about nine feet around. We had to have three astronauts in it, and they're squeezed in pretty tight, but you imagine that would be the case in such a vehicle."

Zimmerman, who is a veteran of twenty-fourth century starship design, explains what influenced the look of this first twenty-first century vessel: "It was driven partly by the script requirement to use a ballistic missile as the vehicle to launch the first warp ship into space. We started with that, assuming that to get into space with this vehicle we would use a leftover missile from the Third World War. Illustrator John Eaves and I worked on what the missile capsule would look like, figuring we had to put it where the warhead would have been. Basically, it's more twentieth century than the 400-years-later kind of thinking that we normally associate with *Star Trek*. It's got buttons and dials and the interior looks a lot like the cockpit of a 747. It was a real chal-

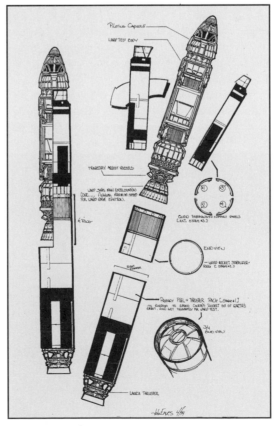

Above: *The* **Phoenix** *ready for warp speed.* **Left:** *Design detail showing how the* **Phoenix** *is housed inside the Titan missile.*

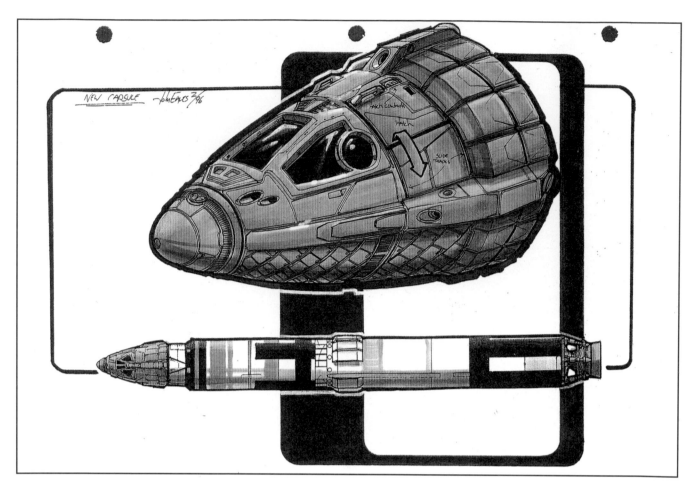

This page and opposite: *The Phoenix's cockpit. A nose cone mock-up was placed atop the actual Titan missile on location.*

lenge, because it was an opportunity to put a design into an interim phase between 'now' and the imagined future that we've created in *Star Trek*, and try to show a logical progression."

This progression almost seems to flow across the centuries in time with the various stages of the rocket's deployment: "The script called for the shields on the exterior of the last stage of the missile to fall away, revealing the warp engines which deploy. The miniature work had to be very carefully done to show the movement of the warp engines outward from what is basically a tubular space vehicle. We took that opportunity to do a nod in the direction of Matt Jeffries' starship design for the original television series, and you'll see that those engines resemble greatly the engines on the very first *Enterprise*."

Perhaps the most exciting design work produced for *First Contact* was the creation of the newly commissioned *Sovereign* class *Enterprise*-E. "The new *Enterprise* is a leaner, meaner machine," says Zimmerman. "It's not as family-in-space oriented. It's more a military exploration ship. It's certainly got more firepower than any previous starship. I think it's prettier to look at, too. That's probably a biased opinion. Again, John Eaves, the illustrator, worked very closely with me on it. Most of it is his hand and my head working together."

"I consider it a great honour to be able to do it," says John Eaves, who reveals that he wanted the exterior of the new *Enterprise* to be as photogenic as it was attractive: "From a design standpoint, the *Galaxy* class *Enterprise*-D was really neat. But from a model standpoint, photography-wise, there are a lot of angles you can't film it from, even though it's a really beautiful ship. I thought that if I ever got to design a ship, I would make it so that no matter where you film you're going to get a good angle. So when they called and said they needed an *Enterprise*-E, I thought 'great' — I already had some ideas lined up."

These ideas dated back to October 1995, so that by the time the feature film's art department was officially geared up in January, Eaves already had a basic outline and profile for the new ship. His concept evolved from a single cue in the script: "The script says, 'The new *Enterprise* sleekly comes out of the nebula', and that's about the only thing we had to go from. So Herman [Zimmerman] said, 'Try what you like.' I did a couple of early drawings, and the

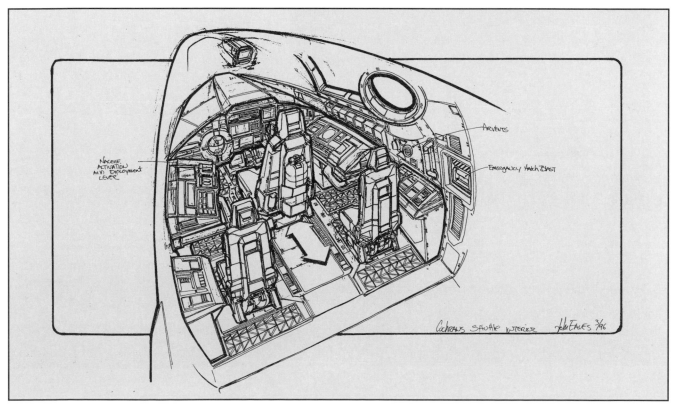

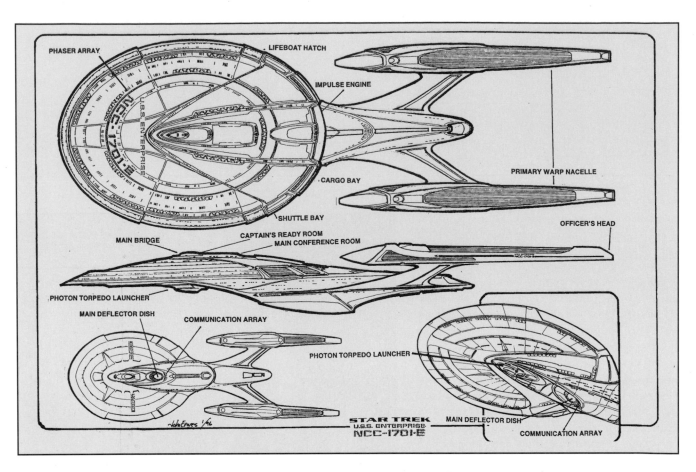

PHASER ARRAY

LIFEBOAT HATCH

IMPULSE ENGINE

PRIMARY WARP NACELLE

CARGO BAY

SHUTTLE BAY

OFFICER'S HEAD

MAIN BRIDGE

CAPTAIN'S READY ROOM

MAIN CONFERENCE ROOM

PHOTON TORPEDO LAUNCHER

MAIN DEFLECTOR DISH

COMMUNICATION ARRAY

PHOTON TORPEDO LAUNCHER

STAR TREK
U.S.S. ENTERPRISE
NCC-1701·E

MAIN DEFLECTOR DISH

COMMUNICATION ARRAY

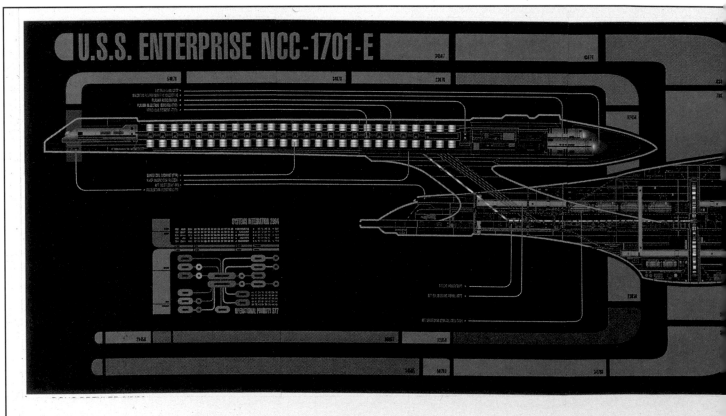

U.S.S. ENTERPRISE NCC-1701-E

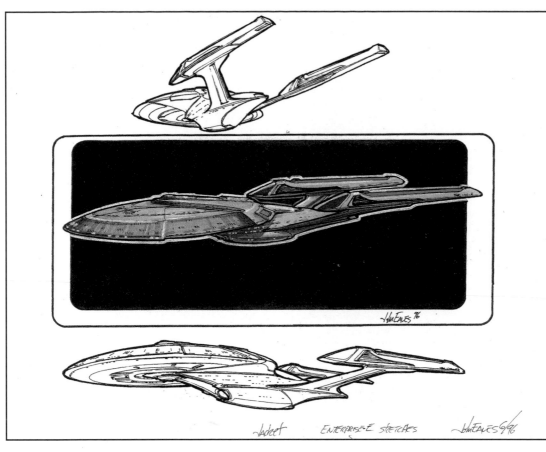

Opposite and left: *John Eaves'* production sketches for the new Enterprise. *He wanted a design that would photograph well from any angle.*

Below: *Cutaway of the twenty-four deck* Sovereign *class* Enterprise.

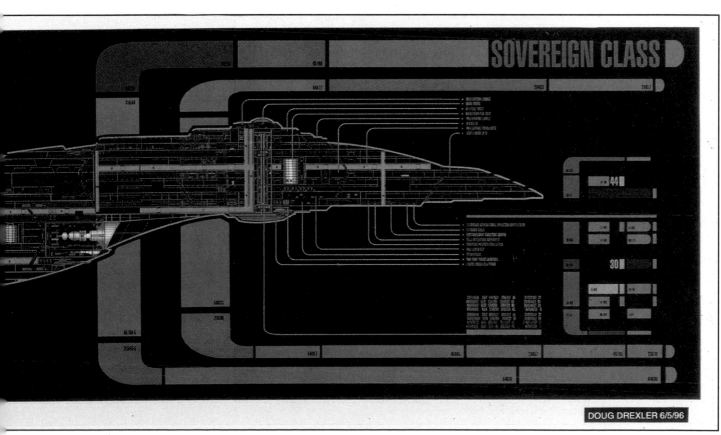

SOVEREIGN CLASS

DOUG DREXLER 6/5/96

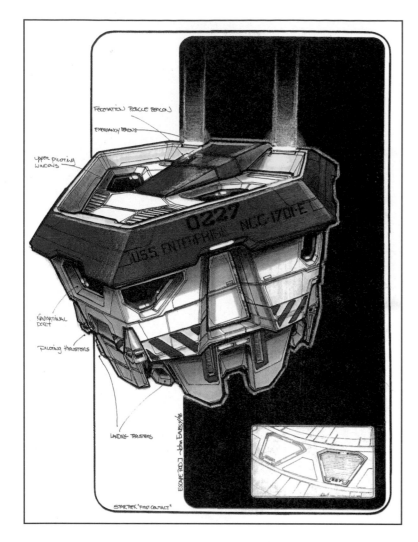

Labels on escape pod sketch:
FORMATION RESCUE BEACON
EMERGENCY BEACONS
UPPER PILOTING WINDOWS
NAVIGATIONAL PORT
PILOTING THRUSTERS
LANDING THRUSTERS
ESCAPE POD — John EAVES 3/96
STAR TREK "FIRST CONTACT"

0227
U.S.S. ENTERPRISE NCC-1701-E

basic shape was something we liked right away. After that, it was just a matter of finessing the lines to please everybody, especially Rick Berman. I wanted to make it real sleek, real fast and structurally a little more sound. I thought this will be able to sustain warp drive a lot easier at a higher speed, just because its shape would be able to maintain the stress and the load."

As the sixth starship to bear the name, the *Enterprise*-E clearly springs from a historical design lineage. "I thought I'd combine something from the *Enterprise*-D, the *Enterprise*-A, the original, all my favourite elements," says Eaves, "so I took a little bit of everything I liked and composed the ship. I wanted to go smaller, between the C and the D scale. It has twenty-four decks, so it is smaller." The previous *Enterprise*, the *Galaxy* class D, had forty-two decks. "The E is longer," explains Eaves, "but mass-wise it's way smaller than the D; it has probably half the D's number of crew. I went back with the longer nacelles — we went short with it and it didn't look right. I

Above: *Design for the* Enterprise *escape pod.*
Right: *Various detailed sketches were made to help the model makers. Here is the deflector array.*

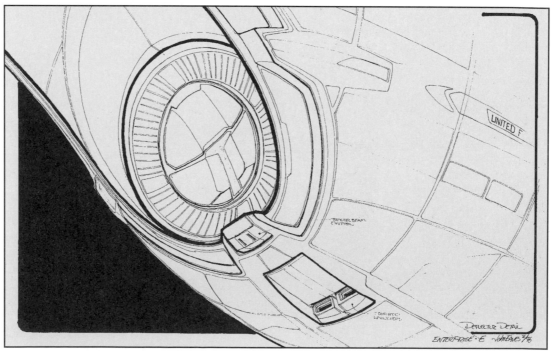

UNITED F
DEFLECTOR DETAIL
ENTERPRISE-E JohnEAVES 3/96

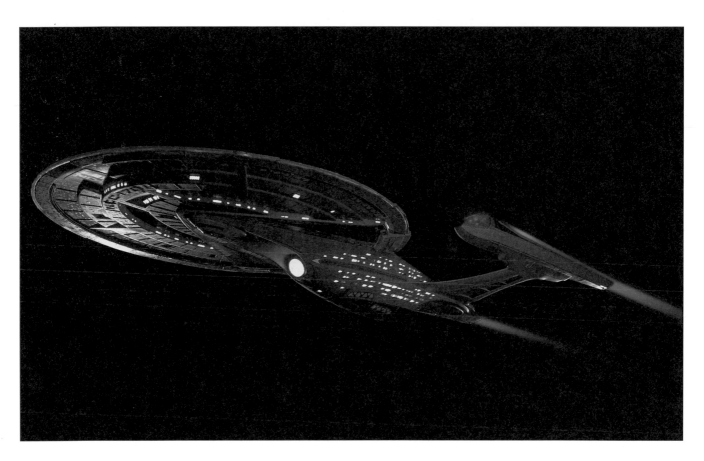

didn't want to go back to the older style, so there's a new form of nacelles."

The new *Enterprise* bears more than a passing resemblance to the *Intrepid* class *U.S.S. Voyager*, designed by Rick Sternbach for *Star Trek: Voyager*. "It was funny," says Eaves. "I was not familiar with the *Voyager*. I had not seen the show or been over to their art department. So when I did my body lines I started looking at the *Voyager* — Rick Sternbach sent over some of his photos for graphics — and I thought 'Oh, man!' From a profile point of view, without the nacelles, it's very similar in shape. I had always wanted to work with an oval saucer going forward because it just seemed 'faster' to me. Rick had used a diamond oval, and I thought it was really neat. The similarity was an accident."

Eaves' design rushed through the approval process with ease until the final stage: "We got to the point where it was almost done and they said, 'Wait, we've only seen this one, let's see a variance to make sure this is what we want.' So I drew all these other ships around that, but they came back to the first one!"

Eaves' workload also included designing the Vulcan ship, various props and the new Borg sphere. To help shoulder this load, Senior Illustrator Rick Sternbach detailed the new *Enterprise*'s hull and prepared blueprints for the miniature to be built by ILM's model shop. "Rick started doing the plans since he knows everything really well," says Eaves. "He'll say, 'We need thrusters here,' or 'The core drop has to be here' — really specific details. So all in all the design went in a big circle: myself, Herman, Rick Berman,

Above: *An early publicity shot of the sleek new* **Enterprise-E.**

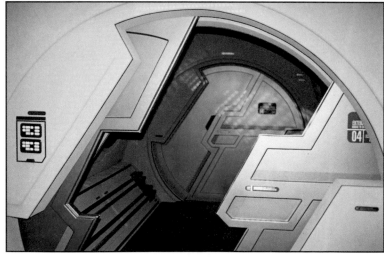

Rick Sternbach and Mike Okuda would come over and interject stuff. So there's a lot of help and support behind the design, which I thought was really wonderful."

"It was something of a round-robin between myself, John and ILM," recalls Rick Sternbach. "John was doing perspective sketches of selected parts of the ship. He was building a two-foot model for ILM to study. At the same time, ILM was cutting some of their cross section bulk heads and I was doing the five-foot blueprints, which they would blow up to ultimately produce a ten-foot miniature. I ended up talking with John about specific parts. We agreed on a certain number of decks, given the size of the ship that Rick Berman had approved, and then it became a matter of deciding what do the lifeboat hatches look like, what do the phasers look like...

"Working with John, we had a great time creating all the little details that go on a starship hull. A lot of the elements were very easy because we just had to transfer them from the *Enterprise*-D to the *Enterprise*-E. But since John had put such a beautiful streamlined spin on the design, it had to get a little more curvilinear, but still look Starfleet. Things like some of the sensor strips — instead of being a very tight row of little squares, they now had to be curved and divided up with a series of curves. Every element of the *Enterprise*-E design had to have a new spin. But you don't mistake this ship for one belonging to any other race we've ever seen.

"I went through a process that was not unlike the one we did with *Star Trek: Voyager*," continues Sternbach, "where once we knew the planned use of the sets for the *Enterprise*-E, we could integrate them into the blueprints. ILM would then be able to sculpt corresponding shapes that you would believe were the places that they were showing on the soundstage, so

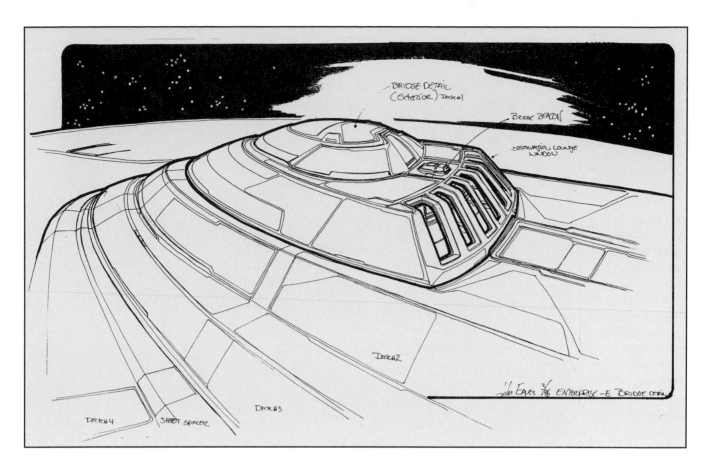

consequentially the shape of bridge on the model looks like the shape of the bridge set. Some of the window shapes are the same on both the sets and the miniature. We had to push and pull some of the shapes, and ILM had to tweak some of the hull contours, but I think overall it turned out to be a very, very handsome vessel."

The most exciting aspect of any new starship is, of course, the bridge. This time, the script called for a new concept in the way the command post was organised, as Herman Zimmerman explains: "It's got a bridge that's described in the script as having all the lieutenants facing the Captain, unlike the triumvirate with Worf in the background on the bridge of the *Enterprise*-D. It's really Picard and everybody else. It has all the same elements of the helm and navigation, which we call ops and conn, but it's a wider bridge. I think it's more actor-friendly. I was curious to hear that Jonathan [Frakes] had a little trouble getting used to it, which didn't occur to me since he was in on the design all the way through. But of course he worked on the old bridge for seven years, so obviously it would be a change for him. And again, the bridge and the exterior of the *Enterprise* owe as much to the first *Enterprise* and to the *Enterprise* of the first six films as they do to *The Next Generation Enterprise*. You'll find elements of all three,

and I think the melding is correct for the requirements of the script."

One of the changes from previous *Starships Enterprise* is in the way the large viewscreen is handled. "It has a new viewscreen that's not on unless you ask for the image to be called up," explains Zimmerman. "That's something that we started doing on *Star Trek: Deep Space Nine*. It answers a problem we've had for a long time, which is, 'Is it a window or is it a viewer?'" Although the image on past viewscreens could

Below: *The roof of the new bridge set under construction. Its shape is designed to tie in with the exterior of the model* Enterprise.

This page: *Early designs (one featuring the working title* Star Trek: Resurrection) *showing the new bridge set (right) and how the bridge and observation lounge sets are now physically connected (below).*

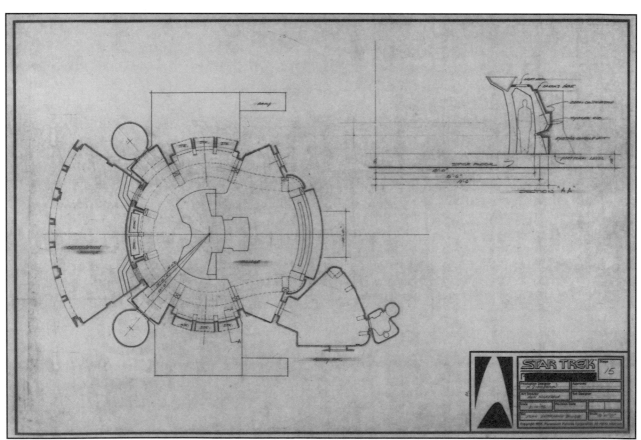

This page: *The Enterprise-E's bridge set during construction, inside (left) and out (below).*

shift angles or magnify images on request, the ever-present view of space that occupied the screen unless instructed otherwise lead to this confusion: "That's something that Gene Roddenberry had always wished we could do something about, and we never quite figured out how. And this addresses that. When there's no image, there's just a wall."

In addition to the new viewscreen, the *Enterprise*-E has a few other elements that suggest a technological progression over its predecessors. "We have interface

with our electronic 'wallpaper' that's certainly higher tech than we've seen previously," says Zimmerman. "In the *Enterprise*-D, we didn't use many computer graphics. We didn't have that many television sets to work with. There's probably sixty television sets in the walls of the new *Enterprise* bridge, all of them with various items of information that are moving all the time. It's a really dynamic background for the action. Unfortunately, during much of the picture there's no main power to the bridge, and it's on emergency power, so very little of the background is noticeable."

When it is shown, the information displayed comes under the province of Scenic Arts Supervisor Michael Okuda. "From a graphic point of view," says Okuda, "the most fun part of *First Contact* was coming up with a new *Enterprise* bridge. The bridge has always been the icon of *Star Trek*. Other than the ship itself, it's the thing that most identifies *Star Trek*. Once again, we were trying to balance the desire to keep this a clear descendant of what we did on *Star Trek: The Next Generation* and yet keep it fresh, make it look like it's a little more advanced and a little bit different. We felt a great responsibility not to simply abandon what had come before. So if you look at the

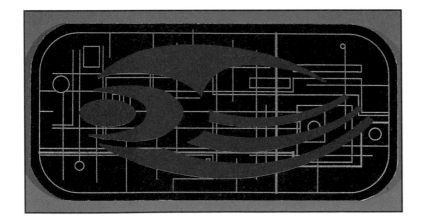

design of the readouts, if you look at the choice of colours and topography, for the most part they're very consistent with what we have done previously. Not only on *Star Trek: The Next Generation*, but also on *Star Trek: Voyager*, on the *Defiant* and the run-abouts on *Deep Space Nine*. There's that very strong family connection. I believe that kind of continuity helps give reality to the *Star Trek* universe in general."

Another key feature in the new *Enterprise* is the engineering set. "It's one of the most impressive sets that we've ever designed for *Star Trek*," says Herman Zimmerman. "It's a three-storey engine room with the largest warp core we've created to date. It's very prominent in the picture, because it's occupied by an alien culture, and it gets transformed into a mechanical storage facility, or 'breeding ground' for the Borg. Much of the final moments of the picture are happening in engineering. Curiously enough, it's sitting in exactly the same spot on the same stage that the other favourite set of mine once sat a few years back: the Klingon courtroom from *Star Trek VI*."

Zimmerman remembers transforming the ship, and engineering in particular, into Borg territory: "We had a lot of practical instruments all over the sets for

Right: *The names on the* Enterprise-E's *dedication plaque won't be visible on screen, but they include Producer Rick Berman and* Star Trek *creator Gene Roddenberry.*
Below: *Hand-held props play an important part in defining the film's 'look'.*

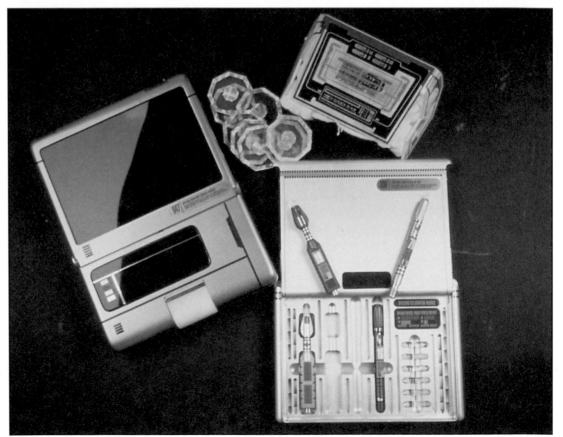

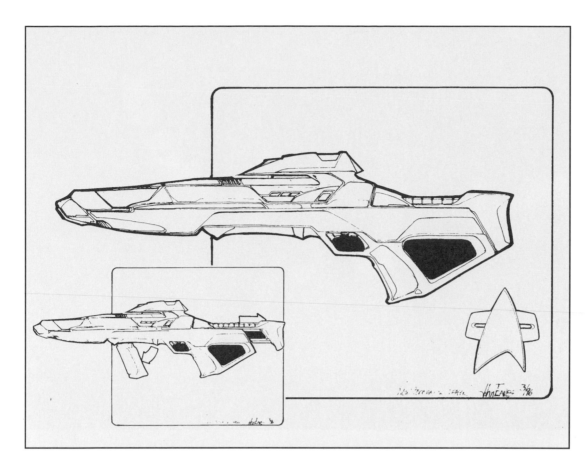

Left: *John Eaves'*
design sketches for
the phaser rifle.
Below: *Starfleet*
issue: heavy duty
phaser rifles are
used against the
Borg.

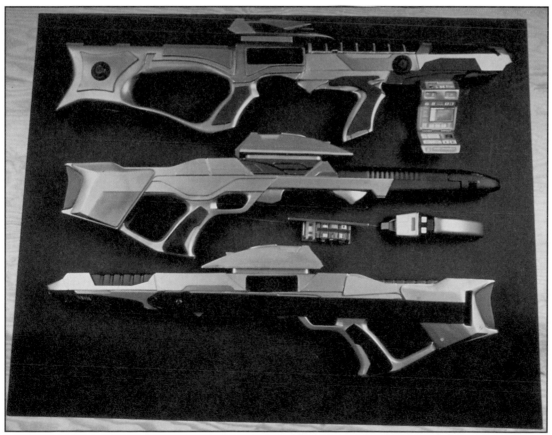

Above: *The warp core.*
Opposite page: *The Borg sphere from initial design sketch to completed model.*
Below: *The observation lounge display case.*

this film. When we Borgified parts of the ship, we used a combination of ordinary fluorescent lights, black lights and fibre optics, in addition to ordinary set lighting, to create the look. The technique that was used was very labour intensive. We had a really wonderful paint crew that gave us fantastic, realistic-looking mechanical walls and props that when properly lit are very believable. One of the problems you always have with building futuristic sets is coming up with something that's unique, and more than that, unique to an alien culture."

While the sickbay is a reuse of the *Voyager* set, the *Enterprise*-E's new observation lounge is a redress of the lounge from the *Enterprise*-D version, now outfitted with a glass display case housing models of the previous starships. "It's an observation lounge that's very similar to the one that we've seen on *Star Trek: The Next Generation*," explains Zimmerman. "It is, however, physically connected to the bridge, which is something we were never able to show on the series. The observation lounge doors lead directly to the bridge, and if you open the door to the bridge and someone walks through, you can actually see the stars out of the window of the observation lounge. We connected the Captain's ready room to the bridge, and we connected an airlock anteroom and actual air lock to the bridge as well."

The new *Enterprise* features one more *Star Trek* first, an addition that will certainly address an indelicate but essential concern of *Star Trek* viewers — a detailed bathroom in the Captain's quarters. "They won't ever show it," John Eaves supposes, "but they even had a little toilet — it's a hexagonal shape!"

Strangest of all the alien hardware is the Borg ship design. While *First Contact* features the traditional Borg cube, it also introduces the new Borg sphere. "The Borg cube is a refinement of the one that was invented for *Star Trek: The Next Generation*," explains Zimmerman. "It's a whole lot more detailed, of course, because for the big screen you need to do that, but the Borg sphere is a new concept. It's like a

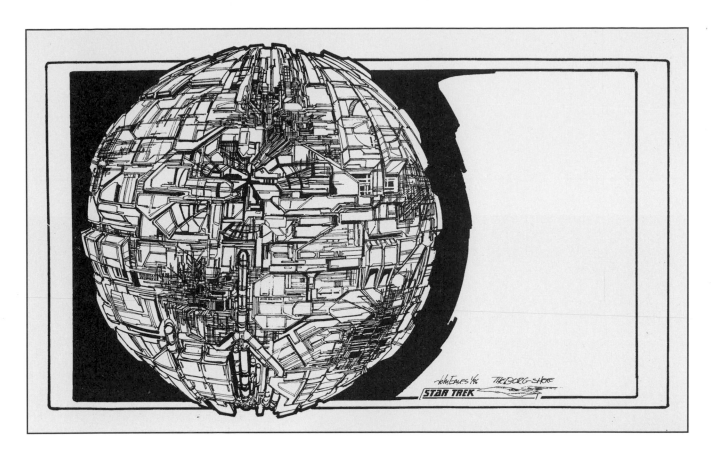

scout ship; in this instance it's used as an escape vehicle."

The Borg sphere came with its own challenges, most notably the danger of comparison to another famous spherical object in science fiction lore. "Our biggest problem was not to confuse it with the Death Star from *Star Wars*," admits Zimmerman, "and I think we managed that successfully. We just made it look completely different. The Borg, of course, have a unique look, and we Borgified that sphere." The look of the sphere itself was in keeping with research from some of Zimmerman's past projects: "I've done a number of science fiction things other than *Star Trek*. I did a remake of *The Invaders*, for instance, for Quinn Martin some years ago. When I was investigating what the best kind of ship would be to invent for that, I asked a lot of scientists — people at NASA, JPL — and they all agreed that a spherical shape is best."

All things considered, Zimmerman feels that *Star Trek: First Contact* presents a rich and detailed look that, combined with a great script, makes this the best *Star Trek* feature to date: "This was the most perfect result I think I will ever achieve in the pre-production and production period of a picture, because the personalities all jived together beautifully. The studio, the cast and crew were delightful. The time allotted for shooting was adequate. We did everything by the numbers, and it all came out right." ∎

COSTUMES

Deborah Everton's costume designs included civilian disguises for the Enterprise crew's visit to twenty-first century Earth.

just tons to do. It was so very quick, with very, very, slight prep time — it's really been running like crazy this whole shoot! But we got it done. I have a great group of people working with me, and somehow or another we pulled it together."

First Contact heralds a rethinking of the Borg from their last appearance on television. Writers Braga and Moore set out to reinvent the deadly adversaries, taking full advantage of the feature film possibilities and making them even scarier than they had been on the small screen. This Borg overhaul carried over into both make-up and costume. Everton made her own contribution to the new Borg look: "I came up

This page and opposite above left: *Deborah Everton's design sketches for the Borg.*
Right: *The Borg as they appear in the finished film.*

Deborah Everton is a veteran of science fiction costume design. She has lent her talents to such films as *The Abyss*, *Highlander II*, *Lawnmower Man 2* and *The Craft*, as well as the pilot episodes of the television series *Earth 2*, *The X-Files* and Paramount's upcoming sci-fi pilot, *The Osiris Chronicles*. It was her work on the latter which was noticed by *Star Trek: First Contact* director Jonathan Frakes. "He was so enthusiastic," Everton says of Frakes' reaction to her work. From there, things moved extremely fast. "I think I met the producers on a Thursday, and that next Monday I was at work!

"The script is so great," she says. "It's a huge scope, with 700 or 800 costumes at least, and that's not counting the multiples." While *Star Trek* veteran Bob Blackman returned to design the new, darker uniforms for the *Enterprise* crew, the overwhelming remainder of *First Contact*'s costumes were Everton's responsibility. "I had everything else," she says. "The twenty-first century villagers, the nightclub, the spacesuits, the Borg, the Borg Queen — there was

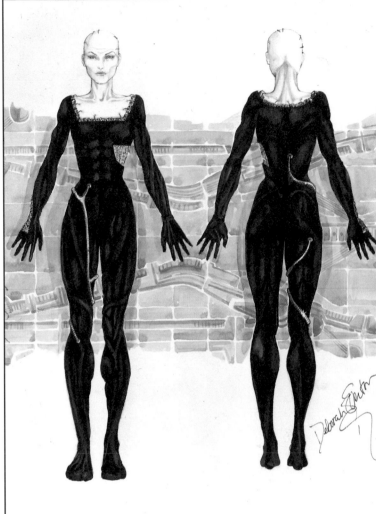

with this concept — a similar silhouette to the old Borg, but much more elaborate for a feature's scope. I wanted it to look like they were Borgified from the inside out rather than the outside in. It was tricky to get the layers and the depth into the costumes so it would look like the piping and the tubing were coming out of them. We collaborated on the headpieces with [make-up designer] Michael Westmore; I'm really happy with them. And when you see them all lit and in their element, they're very creepy."

Central to the newer, scarier Borg is the Borg Queen: "Her whole thing is that she doesn't walk around scaring people or killing people, so I wanted to keep her really simple and elegant. You can do something incredibly elaborate and then the actor can get lost in that, to the point where you miss all

Above right: *Design sketch showing the Borg Queen costume.* **Left:** *The Borg Queen.*

"It's a huge scope, with 700 or 800 costumes at least."

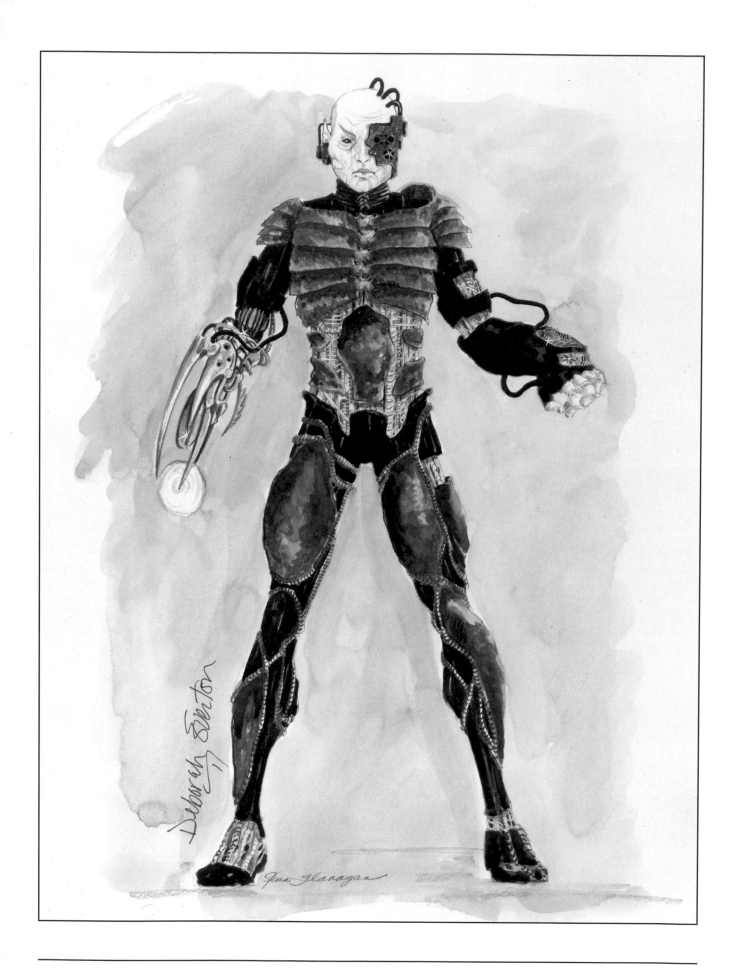

Right and far right: *The original designs for Dr. Crusher's and Picard's twenty-first century disguises.*
Below: *Cochrane's heavy fur coat.*

their nuances." Everton chose a design that was threatening and scary, but simple: "It's a very complicated suit that she's wearing, but it is 'lean and mean'."

In terms of numbers, Everton says the most challenging aspect of her work was outfitting the inhab-

itants of twenty-first century Earth, a job which included the camouflaged *Enterprise* visitors. In achieving the style for the next century, Everton never strayed too far from tonal qualities historically associated with a *Star Trek* film: "The thing about *First Contact* is it's a very optimistic feature. Even after the apocalypse or whatever they've gone through it would still be — not happy, but optimistic is the word. I mean they're cohesive. They have a society. They're not *Mad Max* kind of people — it's more like a Western. I actually patterned their look on Dickens. They really have that sort of Dickensian quality in that they're scruffy but they're not without some society: they have their little gardens, and they have their little bar, of course — a real Wild West town."

Chief among the twenty-first century citizens is Zefram Cochrane. As a key figure in *Star Trek* mythology, the inventor of warp drive, Cochrane's costume had to match his fame. "Cochrane is an eccentric genius, kind of a kook, but he's our hope for the future," explains Everton, "so I wanted to bring out a loveable, quirky quality about him. You don't want somebody who's so repulsive that the audience is going 'yeccch!'" At least one bit of her design proved a cause for gratitude from actor James Cromwell — the heavy fur coat that Cochrane wore. As Cromwell says, "I remember freezing. I was very, very cold. People were blue, but I was quite happy because I had a very heavy coat on, which was part of my character, which I didn't have to take off. So of course, it really didn't matter to me!" Meanwhile, Cochrane's distinctive hat owes its existence to having caught the eye of Producer Rick Berman. Everton laughs about its inclusion: "I had used [hats] as a design concept for that era but never manufactured one. Rick Berman kept liking this hat — every time he would see it on one of the illustrations it was, God, I really like that hat!' So when I made it for Cochrane, I wanted to make it sort of funkier, as a character thing."

Everton's vision for Alfre Woodard's character, Lily Sloane, was equally inspired. "Lily has to be an action girl," Everton says, "and I really wanted to see the transformation from when she's her scruffy little self, the person who props up Cochrane, to the person who puts on this elegant evening gown in the 1940s holodeck scene. So I kept her in her basic colour scheme, but really changed her drastically.

Below left: *Original sketch for Zefram Cochrane's costume.* **Below:** *The holodeck scene allowed Everton to step outside science fiction fashions.*

grubby people — it's not often I get to do dresses and white dinner jackets and tuxedos, and I love that! I'm a girl — I like the pretty dresses!" The stars' fashions, it should be pointed out, were backed with rented and altered outfits for the numerous holo-patrons.

It's very easy to make a spacesuit look bad, very hard to make one look good. Fortunately, Everton came to the problem with some practical experience, having worked on similar designs for the underwater suits used in James Cameron's *The Abyss*: "Any sort of specialised costumes like that are just a nightmare, unless they're actually real. There are all sorts of prob-

Above: *Picard's and Sloane's costumes for the holodeck scene.*
Right: *Design for Lily Sloane.*
Opposite above: *The spacesuit helmet.*
Opposite below: *Everton's design for the Starfleet spacesuit.*

You really get to see her as a multi-dimensional person, as opposed to how you often see women in action movies. Lily has a lot going on, and I wanted people to see that: she could be tough and vulnerable and sexy and beautiful and glamorous and frightened and aggressive."

The holodeck scene, in which Picard and Sloane trick the Borg by employing a 1940s Dixon Hill holo-program, afforded Everton the opportunity to step outside the fashions ordinarily decreed by science fiction. "It was a nice respite from the twenty-first century and the Borg!" she laughs. "When you do science fiction, you're often doing down-and-dirty

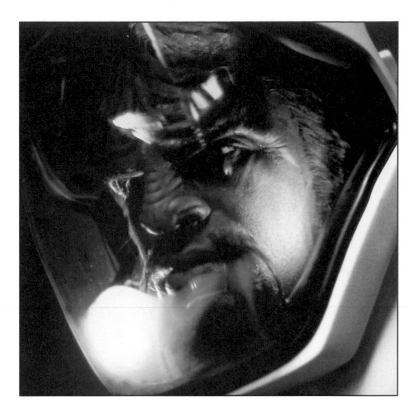

lems that go along with them. They have to do very elaborate things; they have to accommodate flying harnesses, and electronics, which never work. You're always fiddling with it! The challenge for me was to design something that was leaner than, say, a NASA suit or a present-day suit, but would still have enough resonance of [a present-day suit] that the people could identify [with it], so it doesn't alienate the characters to the audience. The other thing was I wanted them to be sexy — they're dashing heroes and I really wanted them to look like that. I also wanted a lot of things that looked like they would strap on and go, 'ka-chunk!' and be beefy, and not look like they're wearing pyjamas or something.

"And those helmets look very simple — but the engineering that went into them was intense! Another lesson I learned from *The Abyss* is how to make a helmet so you can light the actors without it looking obvious and you can see so much of their face. There are tremendous problems — visibility, fogging the lens, the electronics, not asphyxiating the actor, the problem with reflections. And I tried to weight them forward a bit, so they would have an aggressive stance as opposed to a passive stance. But I think we've accomplished everything that we could possibly want to with them, and they definitely look heroic — in that light grey which will photograph white. It's the classic 'our guys' in the white spacesuits against our very dark Borg. I mean, *Star Trek* is like an opera, and you don't want to go too far from what the operatic theme of it is."

Everton admits that she's been a *Star Trek* fan since childhood, when she would stay up past her bedtime to watch the original series: "I would say that *Star Trek* probably so formed my childhood that it also directed my career, because I was a huge science fiction fan as a kid — and I didn't know how many little girls are. But you would have to be a fan of science fiction to have your career end up here, as a designer. If it hadn't interested me I never would have taken the first design job in science fiction — I wouldn't have had an affinity for it. So it has been a fantastic opportunity to work on the movie!" ∎

6

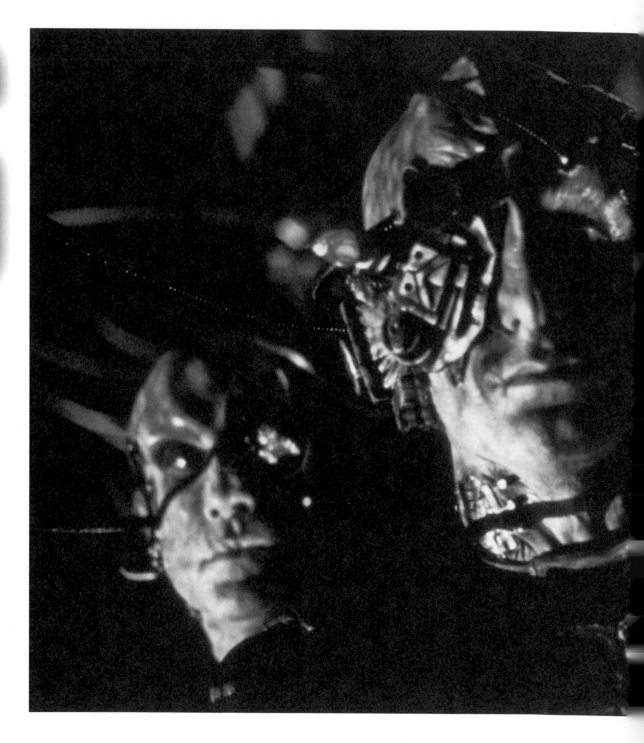

MAKE-UP

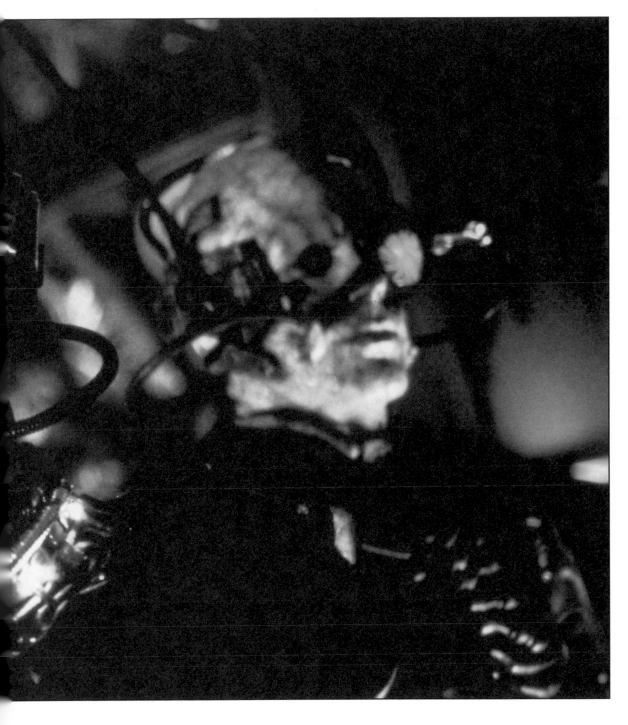

The elaborate Borg make-up for Star Trek: First Contact. We see for the first time the Collective includes Klingons and Cardassians.

Right: *A Borg drone on set.*
Below: *The tools of the make-up artist's trade.*

When *Star Trek* **make-up supervisor and** designer Michael Westmore creates an alien, he casts his eyes to the Earth, mixing and matching his designs from what he sees about him: "I use what's around us on Earth for most of my reference material. Not only animal, but biological [forms], from what's under a microscope to land formations for colour patterns. I take all the magazines that I possibly can: *Reptile, Smithsonian, National Geographic,* kiddie magazines on animals and things. I just really enjoy digging up combinations and putting them together. You think you're looking at something new, but you're not. You're looking at something you're very familiar with." This *modus*

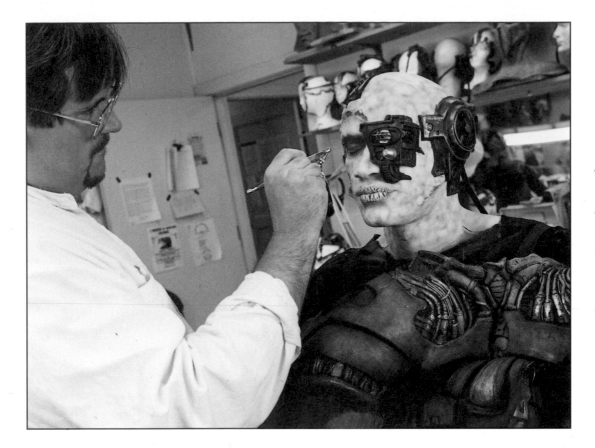

This page: *Each Borg make-up took up to three hours.*

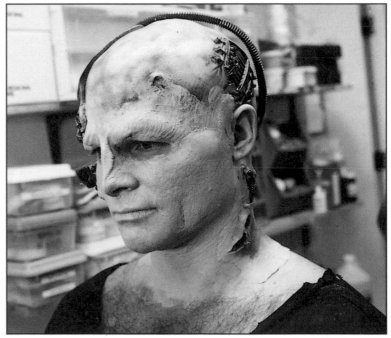

operandi accounts for the success of the many alien races Westmore designs, creatures which don't exist in reality, but nonetheless project a believability of form suggesting they could.

There is something comfortingly familiar about even the fiercer species' physiognomy. However, this approach does not hold true for that deadliest of *Star Trek* opponents, the half-humanoid, half-machine Borg. As a race that has suppressed its individuality in favour of a group link, whose bodies are riddled with hideous artificial implants of piping and circuitry, the mere sight of the Borg sends a chill up the spine. There is something unnatural, uncanny, unholy about their ghastly appearance. With the newly designed look of *Star Trek: First Contact*, they are ghastlier still.

Providing an armada of Borg to overrun the *Enterprise* is no easy task, as Westmore explains: "Our entire time was spent on it every day, even while the television series were in production. I didn't get the script until after the first of the year, and we didn't

"The mere sight of the Borg sends a chill up the spine. There is something unnatural about their ghastly appearance."

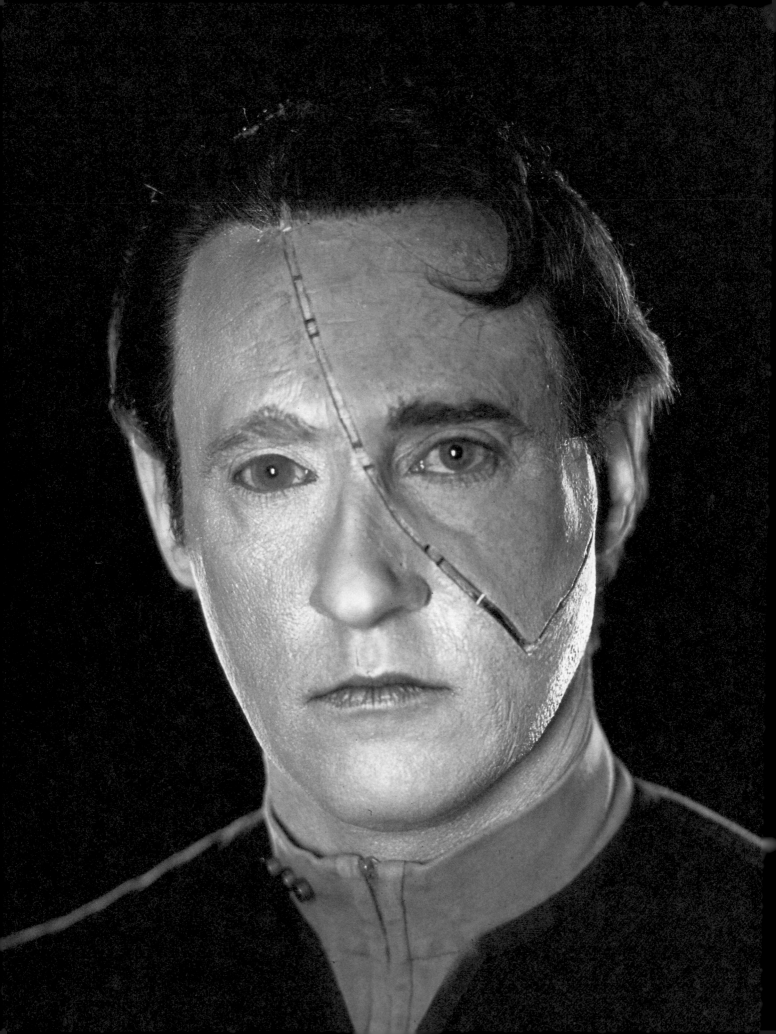

get some Borg designs until the end of March, so I very quickly had to get everything going. It wasn't like you could sit down and design twenty-five Borg looks and have the time to do it."

Initial budgets called for three dozen plus Borg. Although that figure was later reduced, Westmore still had to devise a method of dealing with the tremendous workload necessary for providing unprecedented numbers of Borg. Ordinarily, each Borg actor would have a separate Borg head cast specifically for him or her. This time, however, Westmore's make-up crew sculpted pieces that could be mixed and matched in a full wrap across the back of the head from ear to ear, or used in half and quarter wraps (both rightside or upside down), with eye pieces and other Borg accessories adding more variety. Every Borg actor wore a cast bald scalp rather than the standard flexible bald cap. This allowed the

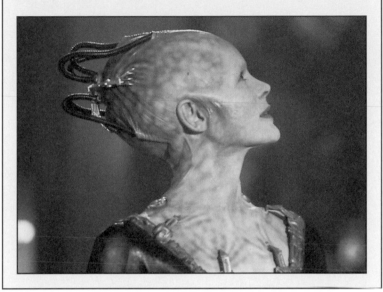

James Cromwell on the Borg: "*The Borg are the ultimate in the darkness that the universe will create for us: a half-organic, half-machine, totally rapacious, totally other* inimical *society bent on the assimilation of all other life forms for no other purpose but to have it all, totally consumed by selfishness and suspicion and power. Sounds a lot like us actually.*"

addition of input jacks that were sculpted into the scalp, which enabled the familiar tubing and cables to be plugged in as called for.

These interchangeable pieces meant the eye pieces and other Borg add-ons could display an even greater diversity in their appearance. "And this took days and days," says Westmore. "One man alone, Barry Koper, sculpted up the Borg eyes; we had ten different kinds of eye. Jake Garber sculpted up all the mechanical Borg pieces for the head implants. Scott Wheeler sculpted up the Queen's head and the bald heads. None of the Borg [actors] had shaved heads. They all had appliances on their heads, and then the other pieces had to go on top of them. There were all the implants that would literally be nailed right into their skin, and pull and warp it. And then there were other individual implant pieces that went on the top of the head, and plates of warped skin with the computer effect showing through them — dangerous things... different appliances with a look like the tubes were buried under the skin where you could still see the ridges disappearing."

Ordinarily, making up an actor as a Borg for television is a process that takes one hour for make-up

Opposite page: *One of the film's most striking make-up effects: the Borg Queen's 'gift' of human flesh to Data.*
Above: *The make-up for the Borg Queen's head was sculpted by Scott Wheeler.*
Left: *Applying the Borg implants.*

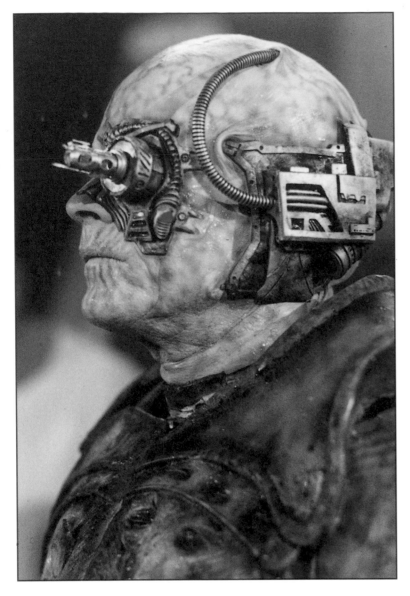

and an hour and a half for costume. This process in *First Contact* became three hours of make-up followed by two hours getting into costume, all of this before a shooting day of fourteen or more hours. Due to the exhaustive nature of the project, an individual Borg drone's look would often be duplicated on a second actor if that Borg were required to appear in a scene two days in a row: "I actually had two teams. We normally ran eight Borg a day, and I had eight make-up artists that would come in around two o'clock in the morning and get the Borgs ready. Then I had another team of eight make-up artists that would come in at three in the afternoon. They would take over on the set and keep them all up, and then take them out of their heads at night, clean up anything that was usable for the next day and have it ready for the artists that were coming at two o'clock. We went on like this for a month once we got into the Borg scenes. It was very exhausting, not only for the actors but for the make-up artists also, to keep those kinds of schedules."

The assembly line construction of the Borg ran through the entire course of Borg shooting: "Scott Wheeler and Jake Garber and James MacKinnon would sit and paint a bunch of bald heads, so those were all done ahead of time. And then Brad [Look] would paint all the metallic ones up, and the pieces

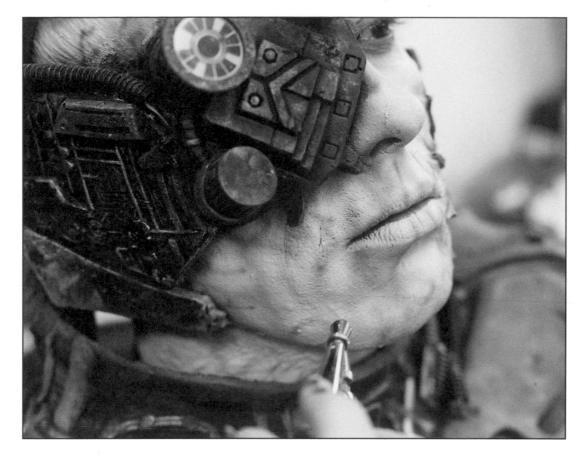

were all set up on Styrofoam heads, and then in would come the Borgs and they'd just start grabbing [rubber prosthetic] pieces. They used up so much stuff that every day we had to run rubber — load the ovens up and cook more rubber. They were gobbling it up faster than we could produce it!"

Despite, or perhaps because of, the gruelling schedule, the make-up team's creative juices really began to flow as more and more Borgs were pumped through Westmore's assembly-line process. The result was a subtle shifting in Borg appearance that actually suggests they are becoming more intimidating as the action of the film heats up. "You'll find they evolved through the shooting of the feature," says Westmore. "When we first see the Borg come into the nightclub [during the holodeck sequence], they look great. But by the time you see them in the hive, the early ones are simplistic compared to the later ones. All of a sudden they're much more ferocious than the earlier ones, much scarier. What happened was — the make-up artists got bored! They got bored putting one tube onto the face. So all of a sudden they were using two tubes, and then they were using three tubes, and then they were sticking tubes in the ears and up the nose!"

Fortunately the work load was eased when the initial order of thirty-five to forty Borg was cut back

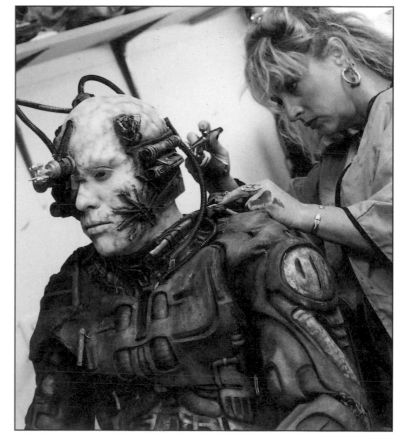

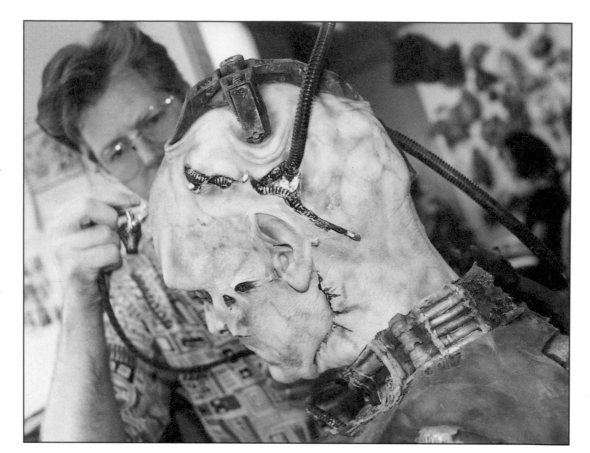

This page:
The Borg head pieces were designed to show tubing and circuitry disappearing beneath the skin.

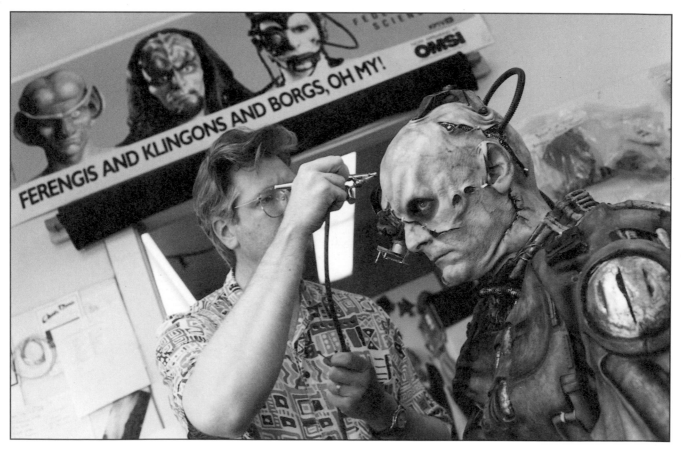

"A subtle shifting in Borg appearance actually suggests they are becoming more intimidating as the action heats up."

to around eight. "They realised that if you had too many in these dark corridors, you won't see anything," explains Westmore. "You'd just see a bunch of bodies moving around and you wouldn't see any definition. So it worked out perfectly — you never felt like you were being cheated."

Leading this fierce horde is the Borg Queen, a subtle combination of circuitry and sensuality: "We

didn't want to do anything that had ever been done before, so nobody could come along and say, 'Ohhh, that looks like *Alien*' or 'That looks like so-and-so.'" Actress Alice Krige won Westmore's admiration for her stiff upper lip when it came to dealing with the rigours of being Borgified, everything from an uncomfortably tight costume to the pain of silverised contact lenses. "She never complained," Westmore

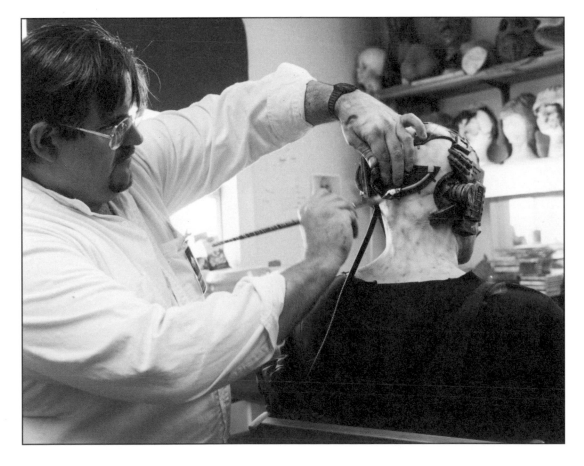

Left: *A delicate process: the finishing touches were applied by paintbrush.*

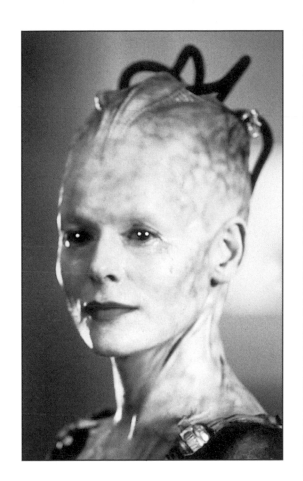

claims, "never said she couldn't put the lenses in any more, never complained about having to get up early. When it finally got down to Data and the Queen working in the hive, it was long days — day after day. Brent and she were so wonderful to work with." Westmore attributes the success of the Queen as much to Krige as to her look: "There had to be a lot of human qualities in the Queen, and her performance is so good — I mean, she sells it! — as this person who is a combination of mechanics and human. Scott Wheeler was basically in charge of sculpting that up. He did a wonderful job, the look that he got. He also made her up. When they first said who it was, everybody really wasn't familiar with anything Alice had done recently. But boy, once she came on stage

Alice Krige's Borg Queen make-up: As the Borg Queen, Alice Krige underwent an excruciating make-up process, yet she thoroughly enjoyed the experience: "In total, the whole thing took seven hours to put on the suit and make-up, and it took two more hours to get out of it. In fact, I had a wonderful time because the make-up artist, Scott Wheeler, who created it, and Mark Bussan, who helped Scott put it on, were wonderful." This sense of fun surrounded her for the entire process of becoming a Borg: "It was a delightful group of people to be surrounded by. Usually, I go into hair and make-up for forty-five minutes and then I'm out of there. For some reason my make-up and hair usually stays, so I don't need maintenance during the day. That's it. I get to spend all the time I need alone on a set. But on First Contact it was a totally unique experience. You know those sharks that are surrounded by little shoals of fish? I was constantly surrounded by about six people. The make-up was always needing to be touched up and repaired, the suit needed gluing and the battery packs needed checking, so I was constantly surrounded. They were all delightful, which is what made it okay." Perhaps having this constant entourage helped Krige step into the role of the Collective's Queen? "That hadn't occurred to me," she laughs, "but maybe it helped on a subliminal level."

This page: *The completed Borg.*
Opposite left:
A Cardassian Borg.
Opposite right:
Picard's nightmare: Locutus and the Borg Queen.

and she turned it on, she was great."

The movie also marks a long-overdue first for the Borg. Previously, all Borg appeared to have been created from the bodies of human or human-like entities. For the first time, *Star Trek* fans will get to see Borg created from other species. Among the new recruits to the Collective, watchful fans will spot Klingons, Vulcans and Bolians, among others. "One day for the fun of it, when I came in they had thrown some Bajoran noses on some Borg," Westmore reveals, "so we had some Bajoran Borg. Then near the end, I asked Rick [Berman] about letting me do a Cardassian Borg. You have to look quick for him because he only worked two or three days."

Less likely to be identified by even the most astute fans, but destined to be a classic piece of *Star Trek* trivia, are the interesting patterns flashed by the Borg's blinking 'chaser' lights on their distinctive eye pieces: "Every eye blinks out somebody's name in Morse code. My son, Michael Jr, is the one that wired and built the programs for the eyes. He's an editor now on *Star Trek: Deep Space Nine*, but he had his time off, and he's always done the electronics for *Star Trek*. We had

thirty-five eyes and there were thirty-five names he programmed into them: Rick Berman, [Paramount studio chief] Sherry Lansing, all the executives. They don't know it, but their name is blinking out in Morse code in some Borg's eye walking around there. He finally ran out of names, so his dog Bonnie is in a blinking Borg eye too!" In fact, Data's head spells out "Resistance is futile!" Additional in-house humour came from sculptor Jake Garber, who worked Berman's name and the phrase "Westmore's barbecue" — the topic of conversation that day — into the computer language cast into each Borg's head. "That's what happens when make-up artists get punchy!" says Westmore with a laugh.

Coming from the third generation of the legendary dynasty of Hollywood make-up artists, Michael Westmore has had a varied and distinguished career, receiving an Academy Award for his work on the film *Mask*. He has received eight Emmy awards, including two for *Star Trek: The Next Generation* and two for *Star Trek: Deep Space Nine*, from a total of thirty nominations, and was Oscar-nominated for both *2010* and *The Clan of the Cave Bear*. Westmore also

wrote the respected study, *The Art of Theatrical Make-up for Stage and Screen*, and was co-author of *Star Trek: The Next Generation Make-up Effects Journal* (with Joe Nazarro).

Though Westmore has a list of credits as long as your arm, he says he's happy to be working on *Star Trek* full time: "I have done some interesting films like *Raging Bull*, and all the *Rocky* films, and the film *Mask* with Cher, and *Roxanne*, and *Masters of the Universe*. There are quite a few that I've enjoyed over the years that I've been involved with, and they were all individually unique in their problems, but nothing has given me the satisfaction and the tremendous amount of creativity that we have here on a daily basis. It never stops here. I don't have time really to do anything but *Star Trek*, and that's fine with me." ∎

"Nothing has given me the satisfaction and the tremendous amount of creativity that we have here on a daily basis."

THE SHOOT

Gates McFadden, Neal McDonough and Michael Dorn filming on the LA soundstage that housed the Enterprise *sets.*

Right: *Alfre Woodard.*

Below: *One of the stunt team in action.*

Principal photography for *Star Trek: First Contact* began on 8 April 1996. The twelve-week production started when the cast members reunited 146 feet below the surface of the Earth, inside the fifteen feet thick walls of a Titan II missile silo. The Titan Missile Museum, a U.S. Air Force installation in Green Valley, Arizona, that actually houses a deactivated Titan II missile, was utilised as the site of Zefram Cochrane's ship, the *Phoenix*.

"That was quite amazing," says Director Jonathan Frakes, "because it was a set that couldn't have been built for millions of dollars. To actually have the missile with all of its rivets and colours and the wiring and tubes and metal and flavour and look (enhanced

by Leonetti's lighting) was just a marvel. It's a pretty phenomenal set." Frakes credits the Air Force with the generosity of letting *Star Trek* shoot there in the first place, which allowed for what is a dynamic sequence in the film. Once in, however, the missile silo presented unique problems in the demands it placed on the film-makers. "It was restrictive," laughs Frakes. "There was one elevator that carried three people at a time down to the base of the missile where a lot of this takes place, and there wasn't much space to move around in. Shooting inside the missile silo was challenging for the film crew. You've got 100 people trying to make a movie that have about two feet of working area around a thirty foot missile."

As our team enters the upper level of the missile silo in the film, Lily Sloane fires a gun up at them. Data, as the only one who can, casually steps off the upper platform and drops down to disarm her. This dynamic sequence was accomplished by stunt co-ordinator Ron Rondell: "We dropped Brent Spiner's

stunt double about eighty feet straight down onto a steel ring, which is a mounting ring for the rocket. Then from there, he jumps down to the ground and Lily shoots at him coming down and hits him the whole way. That was what we call a 'descender'. The stunt man actually jumps off and the wire just free-wheels off of a spool. We control it with the fan blade beating against the air. That keeps him in that position all the way down. And then a brake is applied and stops him right on the ring. The actual unit was completely outside the silo, mounted on the back of a truck. We had a great deal of cable that ran over. All the rehearsals and the cable testing were done on counts and stop marks, which were then put on the cable. When he actually stepped off, the man in the truck who was working the brake, when he saw the stop marks coming, he slowly squeezed on the brake and we set him right down on the top of the steel ring."

It should be stressed that the stunt man in question, Andy Gill, landed safely. No paddings or inflat-

Above: *Director Jonathan Frakes with James Cromwell.*
The following two pages: *The twelve-week shoot's locations included the Angeles National Forest.*

"We dropped his stunt double about eighty feet straight down onto a steel ring, which is a mounting ring for the rocket."

able cushions were used to break his fall. "Because Data's an android, it's nothing for him to jump that far," explains Rondell. "We tried to make it as spectacular as we could. Andy did it several times. At one time, he carried a hand-held camera and photographed Lily, with his feet in the shot, while she was shooting at him from the bottom."

It was here that Patrick Stewart stepped back into the role of Picard after two years away from playing the character. Finding the Starfleet captain within himself after this time was made doubly difficult, as Stewart's first scenes as Picard were played out of uniform. "It felt a little odd," he says, "when I wasn't wearing my *Star Trek* uniform in the scene. I was in civilian clothes. I had to reach underneath this overcoat that I was wearing, touch my communicator, and say, 'Picard to Engineering. Geordi something something something,' and it felt quite strange. It felt odd. Almost like a half-remembered dream, and I didn't quite know if I was saying it properly." The location shooting also afforded the English actor the opportunity to explore a new section of America hitherto unknown to him: "Overshadowing that whole experience for me was that I drove to southern Arizona, and I drove back alone. I've seen so little of this country. I fly over it, backwards and forwards and up and down, side to side. This time, much to the dismay of the production company who don't like actors going off on their own, I was able to see something of the south western region of the United States. It was the most wonderful two days of travelling."

After the sequences in Arizona, the cast and crew moved to the Angeles National Forest near Los Angeles for two weeks of night shooting to accomplish the scenes set on the surface of twenty-first century Earth. "Until Herman Zimmerman got a hold of it," laughs Frakes, "it was an empty part of the forest. He built a small city. It was the post-nuclear war town that was built around the missile tower in the story. It was full of scientists, survivors of the nuclear war, and farmers. It had a wonderful flavour to it."

A sequence absent from the film is explained by Brannon Braga: "There was a scene where Zefram Cochrane is on the run. He just gets fed up with all this talk about being a hero, and he doesn't want to do the flight so he takes off. In the movie, we stun him and drag his ass back to the ship. But there was a scene that we cut out for time reasons, where he literally gets chased and gets trapped on the ledge of a cliff. He is about to jump, and Counselor Troi has to get on the cliff with him and talk him down. It's a very funny scene, where you've got the psychologist on the ledge with Cochrane. Troi is trying to talk to him and he won't leave, and he threatens to jump. Troi says, 'Fine, jump,' and then she pushes him off the ledge. He goes falling and hits a forcefield that we see Geordi has rigged up. He bounces off the forcefield to safety. It turns out that it was a plan on her part, but it was really surprising when the counselor pushes him off the cliff. That just got cut for time. It was running a little long. We felt we had plenty of Cochrane character bits, so we just cut that out."

Above and opposite: *The holodeck nightclub sequence.*
Below: *First contact.*

This town comes under attack by the Borg, a sequence made horrifyingly real by the pyrotechnics of Terry Frazzee's explosions. Throughout this sequence, actress Alfre Woodard did as many of her own stunts as she could, in order to lend the sequence that extra bit of realism. "It gave us an opportunity to have her right in the thick of things," says Rondell, "and you know it's her. She fired the

machine guns and fell down. We blew the base camp up. They were in [the town] with these big laser hits coming down and Lily was right there. We actually blew a ton of debris up nearby which rained down on them, and then a big propane fireball right across them. It looks like she was right in it, because she *was* right in it."

Rondell credits both the spectacular look and the safety of the actors to Frazzee: "They're our best friends because we work with them and they rig all of the stuff that needs to be done with the pyrotechnics. We had some really nice fireballs and explosions — blowing the tents up and blowing the whole fronts out of buildings, with people running in front and being knocked down."

The cast and crew' next stop was downtown Los Angeles' historic Union Station, which was marvellously transformed into a 1930s nightclub. "These are days that you dream of when you dream of making a movie," says Frakes. "You have hundreds of extras in gorgeous period costumes, special effects, the blowing up of a full eighteen-piece dance band, Patrick Stewart in a tuxedo looking like 007, Alfre Woodard in this gorgeous gold satin gown, the Borg invasion, music, dancing, explosions, all the toys, four cameras at a time, and stunts. It was an exciting sequence to shoot and to be part of."

The 1930s nightclub was part of a Dixon Hill holodeck program in which Picard and Lily hide from the advancing Borg invasion. The station was filled with around 150 extras, supplemented by a team of around twenty-five stuntmen. Stunt Coordinator Ron Rondell took his turn as a holograph as well: "I played the part of one of the henchman guarding Nicky the Nose. I have a little confrontation with Patrick."

In the sequence, Picard grabs Nicky the Nose's machine gun and begins to mow down the Borg. "We had a Thompson sub machine gun, the old Eliot Ness gun, with a full load of blanks," explains Rondell. The 'squib hits', Hollywood-speak for the impact shots on a person hit by gunfire, presented an interesting challenge to the stunt team: "When you see somebody shot in a film, you see an impact on them and blood comes out. But the Borg don't have any blood. We figured we would use spark hits. In that way we'd be able to show the bullets hitting them and shorting them out." As the Borg go down, gun fire tears into the holographic 1930s crowd: "We tore the place up. They were grabbing formally dressed ladies and flinging them over tables full of break away glasses and wine bottles. I was really excited about being able to do that sequence."

The final nine weeks of the production occurred

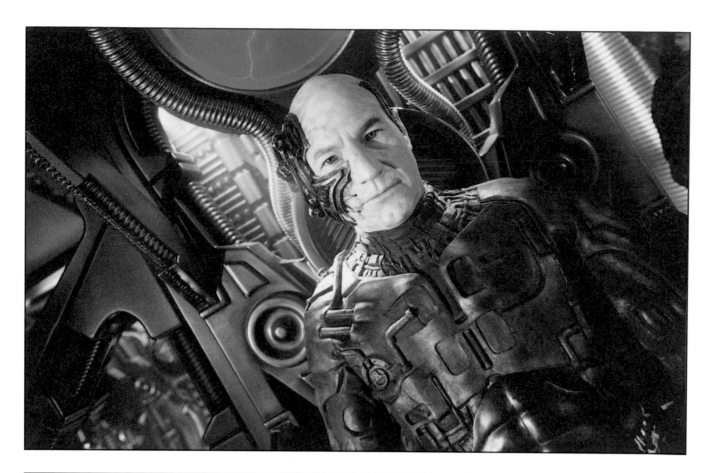

"Inside the hive, Borg are stacked two high, and as the team enters, they spring to life and attack."

on three soundstages at Paramount Pictures. One of these contained the *Sovereign* class *Enterprise*-E's newly designed bridge. Frakes, a veteran of overcoming the difficulties of shooting bridge scenes, praises the virtues of this new space: "The placement of the characters is similar to what we had all gotten used to on the *Enterprise*-D, but Herman Zimmerman has opened the space up somewhat, so it was easier to

shoot than on the other *Enterprise* bridge."

In one sequence, the *Enterprise* crew advances into parts of the ship now thoroughly converted into Borg territory. Inside the hive, the Borg are stacked two high, and as the team enters, they spring to life and attack. "We must have killed probably twenty Borg in there," exclaims Rondell. "We used what we call nitrogen ratchets on some of the impact

Opposite: *Stewart (above) and Dorn (below) in character on the soundstage at Paramount.*
Left: *The Borg hive.*

Above: *Donning the spacesuits.*

shots to pull these Borg completely across the room on a wire cable. It made for a really exciting scene in what is sort of a confined area in the spaceship because of the corridors. You don't have the room that you had in the dance hall which allowed us to be all over the place."

Rondell is full of praise for the enthusiasm of the Director: "Jonathan was great to work for, because he got as excited as I did. If I could fly a guy ten feet, and I'd say, 'Well now, Jonathan, we can fly him further than that,' he'd say, 'Oh? Well, let me see it!' He loved it. It was really a chance to do some big stuff which they don't have the money or the time to do on the series."

One of the most dramatic scenes of the film is when Picard, Worf, and Hawk don spacesuits and engage the Borg on the outside of the ship. A full sized deflector array was created on one of the sound stages for this exciting sequence. This unique topography presented an interesting challenge to Frakes.

"What was particularly difficult about it was that the set itself was circular," he recalls, "so there was no geography that you could relate to. Then the three heroes, Patrick, Neal McDunough, and Michael Dorn, were in space suits with helmets with Plexiglas face plates on them, so from a distance they all looked alike, and the Borg by their very nature look very, very similar."

Rondell tackled staging a battle in zero-G: "We had to fake a weightless condition out there. Terry Frazzee had a terrific rig set for us. We harnessed all our guys in space suits and [harnessed] the Borg. That way we could fly them, although their boots were magnetic. Any time they shot one of the Borg, we just assumed he shorted out and lost his magnetic tie to the ship, and we just floated him off into space." But there's more than one way to fly a Borg. Rondell's team discovered various interesting ways to sail them off into the void: "We tried to do some different things, turning them over and

Brannon Braga on polishing the action: *"We spent a great deal of time on the action sequences in terms of the hull battle outside the ship. We wrote a broad description of events outside the hull, but once we were in preproduction, we went back in and rewrote it to come up with more and more gags, to get more and more specific, and really create and storyboard a sequence that would be very elaborate and exciting."*

pulling them out on what we call a hip pick — a single pick down to the harness at the hip socket — so when we picked them out, they would turn to their side, then upside down, then back to their side as they swivelled and went out into space."

The Borg weren't the only ones experiencing weightlessness. In a desperate gambit, Captain Picard propels himself through space as well: "We had Picard flying completely across the set. He travelled probably 150 feet through the air from one side of the ship dish clear to the other side." This was not a stunt double standing in for the good captain. "He actually did it. He liked it," says Rondell.

Inside the Borg hive, Frakes feels some of the most amazing work of the film occurred: "First, visually, there's Data's confrontation with the Borg Queen, who is a design unto herself thanks to Michael Westmore and Deborah Everton. Then there's the chemistry between Alice Krige and Brent

Above: *Patrick Stewart.*
Left: *Filming the space walk sequence.*

In the final moment of the film, Zefram Cochrane strides forward to greet the Vulcan, humanity's first ever encounter with an alien species: I don't know how to describe it actually," explains James Cromwell. "It's like Lewis and Clark or the first guys who got off the boat in America, or the first Viking who set off and found something. It's a whole new world." Cromwell says that at that moment, he had ceased to be 'acting': "All I had to do was say, 'It's real, it's real, it's real.' And I kept on saying to myself, 'What would it look like? What would I do? Would I perspire? Would I shake?' and I thought, 'God, the real thing is that you don't know what you'll do when it actually happens.'"

Spiner, who worked wonderfully together."

Alice Krige, who gave life to the Borg Queen, thoroughly enjoyed being paired with Spiner. "Brent was wonderful," she says, "because his level of concern for Data was just astonishing. He continued work at the script and the storyline and wrestled with it until the scene was done. He continued to work at it throughout the process, seeking to make it more complex, more real. He was quite, quite wonderful. I was enormously grateful to have him there, because obviously he's steeped in this, and it was just wonderful that I, who am a total newcomer, was

partnered by someone who cared enormously about getting it as good as it possibly could be." While Krige has a great respect for Spiner's professionalism, it was his android counterpart that stole her heart. "I totally fell in love with Data," she admits. "I'm afraid it was head over heels. The character has a naiveté and innocence that I found completely beguiling."

The set of *Star Trek: The Next Generation* was always renowned as a fun set to be on, and the tradition continued with *First Contact*. Krige remembers her first taste of *Star Trek*-bonding: "What was really lovely were the days that Patrick, Jonathan and Brent were on the set together. There was this wonderful sense of hilarity and carnival. They obviously enjoy each other so much, and they tease each other. It was just very funny and really delightful to see the three of them. It was really a very happy experience.

All of the creative people involved have got very unusual imaginations and really were a great deal of fun to be around. I was eventually running on pure adrenaline, because mostly we were working an eighteen hour day, but in spite of that I really had a wonderful time."

Once again, Patrick Stewart performed his own stunts, as the actor was on another wire for the final battle sequence. "We flew him again on wires," explains Rondell, "where he was climbing hand over hand up a big rope trying to get away. The Queen grabs his ankle and is pulling on him and with her weight and his weight, the rope snaps and he swings across the room and lands on a balcony. We flew him in there, and he actually made the swing on his own once too. He's quite athletic. I was quite surprised as it was one of my first times working with him." ■

Opposite left: *The film's moving finale.*
Opposite right: *Jonathan Frakes jokes with a Borg.*
Above left: *The full-sized deflector array created on the soundstage.*
Above right: *Brent Spiner and Alice Krige 'worked wonderfully' in their scenes together.*

"What was really lovely were the days that Patrick, Jonathan and Brent were on the set together."

8

VISUAL EFFECTS

The time-travelling Borg sphere begins its journey. One of over 222 visual effects shots in Star Trek: First Contact.

Photo courtesy of Industrial Light & Magic.

The Borg invade. Time warps. Transporters energise. Spaceships battle and explode. The *Phoenix* launches, carrying humankind into space for its first warp flight. Over 222 visual effects shots were created to make these magical events a stunning reality in *Star Trek: First Contact*. "We had so much work," explains Co-Producer Peter Lauritson, "that I divided things up to have Industrial Light & Magic do a lot of the major optical work, and then for the things that I felt we could do in town, I contracted with people that have done work for us on the television series and the last feature. There are about four other companies that have been involved with this movie. ILM had around 135 shots to do, and then within those four companies, there were another eighty-seven shots. We have Pacific Ocean Post doing some work. A company named Illusion Arts is doing matte painting work. Another company called Matte-world Digital is doing some other matte work for us. VisionArt Design and Animation is doing probably eight pretty intricate shots."

The 135 effects sequences that went to Industrial Light & Magic, known also by its acronym of ILM, fell under the direction of effects supervisor John Knoll. The eighty-seven shots that went to the four local FX houses came in under the watchful eye of

Below: *The new U.S.S. Enterprise made use of slides of the interior sets placed in the tiny windows of the model.*

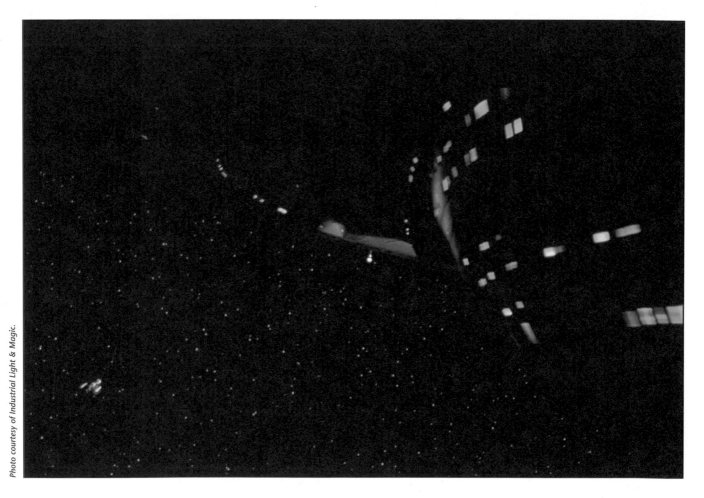

David Takemura, taking a hiatus from his regular position as effects coordinator on *Star Trek: Deep Space Nine* to earn his first feature film credit.

Before any of these visual effects houses could begin to work their movie magic, however, *First Contact*'s other star, the brand new *Sovereign* class *U.S.S. Enterprise* NCC-1701-E, had to be made ready for the camera. The ten and a half foot model was designed by *Star Trek* illustrator John Eaves and built by ILM's model shop, headed by John Goodson. "Since I intended to make the distant views where we're not close up to the model a computer graphic model," John Knoll recalls, "I decided to use the practical model mainly for close-ups. Because of that, I wanted to build it as large as practicality allowed in order to get the best scale. We came up with ten and a half feet as being as big as it could get and still be something that was shootable on our stage. The model had to be light enough that it could be moved around without collapsing under its own weight."

As fans of *Star Trek: Voyager* know, that series' ship was the first *Star Trek* vessel to make use of actual slides of the interior sets placed in the tiny windows of the model. The new *Enterprise*-E uses this technique as well. "I had always thought the lack of scale you get when you just have a flat glowing window was a problem on previous models," says Knoll. "So we have windows that are really transparent with photographs of the interior sets inset at about three-sixteenths of an inch. You get a chance of there being more detail in there; it's not just a flat colour."

"It was a really brutal task to get it all assembled in the amount of time we had to do the work," says Knoll. "Getting all the patterns made, getting the thing built, lit, wired, and painted. It took about two months, about half of what we'd thought was the desired schedule. Building an all new motion-control model that has to have the level of detail and complexity of the new *Enterprise* is a very large task."

Above: *The ten and a half foot* **Enterprise** *model took two months to build.*

"It was a really brutal task to get it all assembled in the amount of time we had to do the work."

In fact, the model team did such a tremendous job that an enlarged, super-detailed matte painting that had been prepared to matte into the sequence where our heroes fight the Borg on the deflector array was not needed. The highly textured finish on the model itself was sufficient to be used in place of a matte.

One of the indisputable highlights of *First Contact* is the opening battle, in which Starfleet engages the Borg in a fight conducted on a scale that would be impossible to realise on the television series' much smaller budget. To bring this exciting conflict to life, an all new three-foot Borg cube was constructed, along with a smaller sphere miniature. The CGI (computer generated image) model of the *U.S.S. Defiant* that had already been created by VisionArts for *Star Trek: Deep Space Nine* was also included. The opening battle also sees the début of three new ship classes, each rendered in CGI. "For the last ten years

we've just been watching the same half-dozen motion-control models," says Knoll, "like the *Reliant* and the *Excelsior*, over and over again. They've built only a few motion-control models, and that's all we ever see. It's implied that Starfleet has a wider spread of different types of ships, but we never see them! So I thought, when we got into these big space battle shots, it would really be nice to see something a little bit different. Since we intended for all the background action to be done with computer graphics anyway, and we needed to build them, why not build new stuff rather than old ones?"

These new starship classes, the *Akira*, the *Steamrunner*, and the *Yeager*, were all designed by ILM Art Director Alex Jaeger. Not only were they each given individual names and 'NCC' registry numbers, but each ship class was approved by Producer Rick Berman, the final authority on all matters *Star Trek*.

Below: *The Borg cube approaches Earth. A new, highly detailed three-foot model was built for the film.*

Photo courtesy of Industrial Light & Magic.

A CGI model of the *Enterprise*-E was also prepared, although its use was mainly restricted to where the story called for it to interact with other particle-rendered CGI elements. This model was also used to achieve the distinctive stretch of a ship moving into warp flight.

As the Borg cube is destroyed in the opening battle, the Borg sphere emerges. It conjures up a vortex in time, disappearing inside to alter Earth's past. John Knoll's team at ILM had to create the look of this time vortex, being careful to tailor their design to what the story needed. "The script requirements dictated a little bit of the look," he says. "The sphere is described as hurtling down towards the Earth's surface and forming this vortex in front of it. Once it's formed, it dives down through. It goes back in time in that moment and changes the past and all of the surroundings change, but the *Enterprise* can't

Left: *The Borg sphere model.*
Below: *The Borg cube under attack.*

Photo courtesy of Industrial Light & Magic.

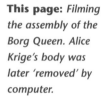

This page: *Filming the assembly of the Borg Queen. Alice Krige's body was later 'removed' by computer.*

be changed because it needs to witness this event. It has to be protected from the change. So the idea was that when the sphere went through the vortex, there would be this large field around it, which envelops the *Enterprise*. That would explain why the *Enterprise* remains unchanged but the universe changes around it.

"At the same time, on the bridge, they don't notice that the whole environment has changed immediately, so we wanted to make sure that whatever this effect was, it was opaque enough to start with so that you really couldn't see the Earth through it. Then, as it begins to dissipate, you see that the Earth has been Borgified. The last story requirement was that it had to appear to be dissipating like this vortex wasn't going to last forever. It's starting to wind down, and they have to hurry up and travel through it before it completely goes away. So based on those specifications, we had some design parameters. It needs to appear in front of the sphere as it's diving down at high speeds. That kind of suggests to me something that looks a little bit like a re-entry plasma effect, but offset out in front of it more. Then, when it dives through, it needed to be able to emit some large field that the *Enterprise* could be enveloped in. That suggested to me something that was like a splash, almost like the sphere landing in water and a big splash coming out and flying back.

"We went with something that has a dense gas, plasma look. It has a little luminance and a little bit of shading from the outside, which then dissipates so gradually it becomes more and more transparent as it's winding down and losing its energy. On the viewscreen, they see this effect dissipating. They see the Earth that's been Borgified to be this polluted, brown surface, but through the vortex they can see the blue Earth. That's our window back in time."

Industrial Light & Magic's new particle renderer, pioneered for *Jumanji*'s animal fur and next utilised in creating *Twister*'s tornadoes, was used to create the corrosive gas cloud released in the Borg's hive in engineering. "You can light the particles and create what appear to be more dense, solid clouds that react to light and shadow, and can cast shadows on themselves and other objects," Knoll explains. "We can do something that looks a little less glowy, something that has a feeling like solid smoke."

ILM also created the 'assembly' of the Borg Queen, when Alice Krige's disembodied head was lowered atop her shoulders and a metallic spine attached to an artificial trunk. Krige's actual body was hidden under a blue-screen drape for this effect. "That was a bit tricky," recalls Knoll, "because it all happens in an unbroken shot. We had to make a transition between a plate of her in a special descender rig to get her to drop down from the ceiling, and

Left: *Captain Picard holds the metallic remains of the Borg Queen.* **Below:** *The Phoenix lifts off.*

another take where she was in her final Borg costume walking forward. We had to do a lot of blends and splits and computer graphic work to get her to be the head and shoulders, fit into the suit, close up, and create the transition into the full body suit."

For the vampiric process by which Borg infiltrate new victims, ILM created animated implants and rendered the skin colourising. The Borg Queen's death sequence was also accomplished by CGI: "There's a prop that was built of the skeleton, a chrome skull and spine that's left after all her flesh has been dissolved away. We've made a computer version of that, and then we scanned her head on a 3-D scanner, so that we had a good representation of the shape of her head. We have a shot where we're taking that head and we're crumpling it down and

Photo courtesy of Industrial Light & Magic.

Andre Bormanis served as science consultant on Star Trek: First Contact, *a position he has filled on the* Star Trek *television series since 1993. During the film, Zefram Cochrane observes the* Starship Enterprise *through a telescope. Bormanis had to work out at what height it would be visible from the Earth, but not too visible:* "I tried to make sure it was a very, very high orbit, because the Enterprise *would be a big object in low-Earth orbit, easy to see. It would be the brightest thing you'd see in the sky. So I had them up in a geosynchronous orbit." For those not versed in the terminology of space, Bormanis explains: "Geosynchronous orbit means that you are 22,000 miles above the Earth, and the period of your orbit is twenty-four hours. The Earth turns once in twenty-four hours, so you'd stay above the same point on the Earth during the entirety of your orbit." Bormanis' main concern was that the* Enterprise *was not so close as to be highly visible to observers without telescopes:* "Given that you're that far out in space, you're a relatively dim object. Something as big as the Enterprise *might be visible to the naked eye, but it wouldn't draw attention to itself, certainly not in a world where there are lots of satellites in orbit."*

then exposing her skeleton, along with the appropriate corrosive burning effect."

At the film's exciting climax, the launch of Cochrane's *Phoenix* warp ship, was accomplished using a motion-control model, combined with shots of the actual Titan missile. "We had to shoot plates for optical work from the very bottom," Co-Producer Peter Lauritson explains. "We were standing right underneath the engines of this rocket at the bottom of the shaft looking straight up, and you could just feel the power of this thing that was hanging above you, and what kind of thrust it would take to lift that thing out of there and take it up into space. We shot just a plate of the mock-up engines that we had to put on the bottom of the rocket, with some light effects which amounted to flashing some red and orange lights on and off to emulate the rocket firing. That would be a plate that ILM would take into their computers. They created a miniature black box version of the bottom of the rocket and did some live-action pyrotechnics where they shot flame and smoke out the bottom of the thing. They shot that, and then they composited that flame and smoke into that plate that we shot, so it would look as if the real rocket fired."

Knoll says he isn't bothered by the idea that rocket launching might invite comparisons to *Apollo 13*: "I don't think of it as a contest really. We're just trying to make a shot that serves the story. Actually, we weren't really looking at *Apollo 13* when we did that work." A more accurate, if less obvious comparison can be made to another blockbuster: "We were globbing onto *Twister*'s R&D [research and design], both for that shot of the silo when the engine starts up, and the exterior shot where you see the rocket fly up. The plume that's coming out of the rocket is the twister upside down with some different shading and behaviour rules. A lot of the R&D that was done to make the clouds of stuff really shade right for the tornado was very directly lifted and used in the plume."

The other special effects houses, each a veteran of the later three *Star Trek* television series, contributed some breathtaking sequences as well.

"There's a prop that was built of the skeleton, a chrome skull and spine that's left after all her flesh has been dissolved away."

Pacific Ocean Post engineered the attack on Cochrane's village, with phaser animation by series regulars Adam Howard and Scott Rader. The film's spectacular finale was split between VisionArt and Matteworld. Josh Rose of Vision Art provided an all-CGI version of the Vulcan ship and its appearance through the clouds, which was based on John Eaves' designs and sculpted model. Backgrounds of the village and starscapes, including the film's final pullback, were composited by Craig Baron at Matteworld. "The Vulcan landing is the end of the movie and the reason why it's called *First Contact*," explains David Takemura, "and we're trying to make that pretty spectacular. It's a very complex shot and almost a couple of minutes long." Meanwhile, the film's stunning opening pullback from Locutus' eye

Below: *The Phoenix prepares for warp flight.*

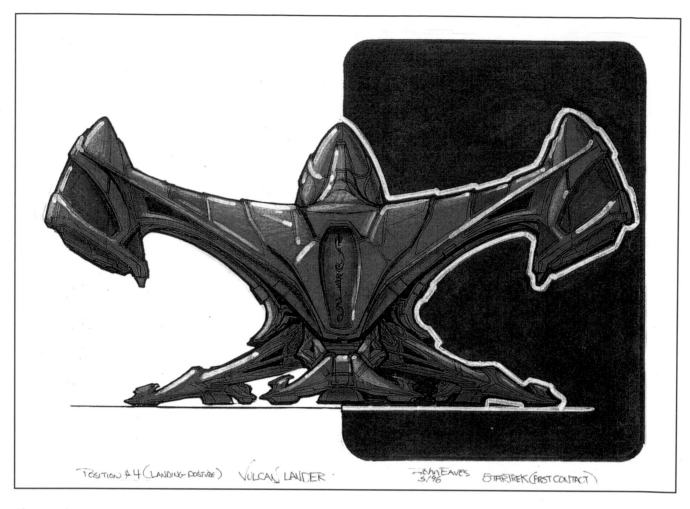

Position #4 (landing-posture) Vulcan Lander John Eaves 5/96 Star Trek (First Contact)

Above: *John Eaves' original design for the Vulcan ship seen at the film's climax.*
Opposite above: *Computer technology was used to erase the actors' flying harnesses in the deflector array battle sequence.*
Opposite below: *'Geordivision' makes it début in Star Trek: First Contact.*
Right: *Concept sketch for the Vulcan ship's landing configuration.*

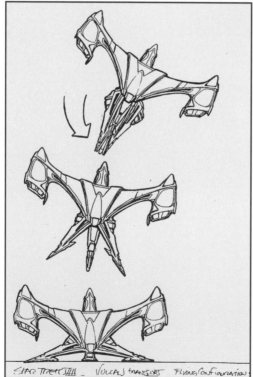

Star Trek VIII   Vulcan transport   Flying configuration

was accomplished by a combination of live action layered over several Borg interior matte paintings by series and features veterans Syd Dutton and Bill Taylor of Illusion Arts. "The camera was almost touching Patrick's eyeball," recalls Takemura. "That's how close it was."

To the delight of actor LeVar Burton, 'Geordivision', as Takemura calls it, also makes its début in *First Contact*. Having dispensed with his VISOR, Lieutenant Commander La Forge now sees with specially constructed artificial eyes. 'Geordivision' refers both to images seen from La Forge's point of view and to the mechanics of his new pupils. It may be amusing to learn the gearing that is seen is based on a sprocket-shaped shower handle Takemura chanced upon at a home-supply store, matted along with some CGI animation onto all-black contact lenses worn by the actor. Takemura also supervised the 'chapter change' at Union Station, where Captain Picard outmanoeuvres the Borg in a Dixon Hill holodeck program, but must switch sections of the novel in order to find the weapons he needs. He also oversaw the erasing of the actors' flying harnesses used to accomplish the weightlessness of the deflec-

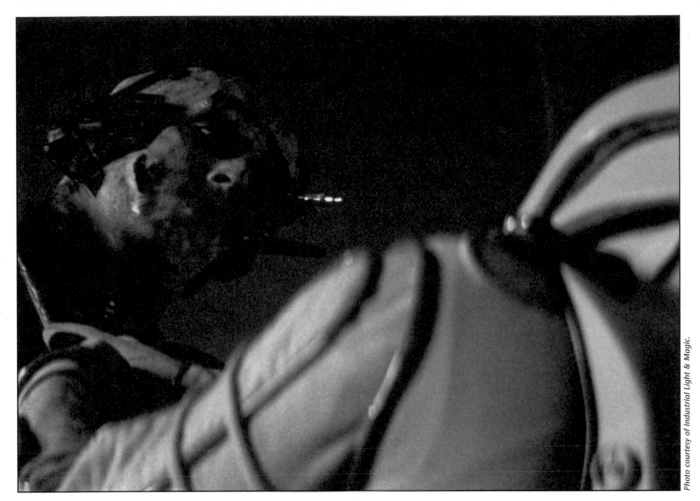

Photo courtesy of Industrial Light & Magic.

tor array battle sequence.

Takemura also worked to create a new look for the transporter beam, building on what has appeared before: "That was my decision — to do something cooler, to add one thing I always thought was lacking in some of the other movies for the transporter effect: a measure of dimensionality, a little more 3D sense of what was happening inside their bodies as they're materialising. So we created some new CG elements at Pacific Ocean Post and added that. I think it makes a big difference in giving the beam-in effect some depth." As to whether or not this new transporter effect will make its way into either television series, Takemura doesn't know. "It's up to the producers and the visual effects producers, but I hope they do. I certainly like it better," he laughs.

As to the overall experience, Takemura says he is exhausted but rewarded: "We had double shifts working day and night, coming in on weekends. It's pretty gruelling, but it's well worth it: my first experience as a feature film effects supervisor, and it's been a great education. Despite the hours, I've had some fun!" ■

9

SOUNDTRACK

Worf commands the U.S.S. Defiant during the Borg attack — a scene made even more intense by the addition of Jerry Goldsmith's music.

Above: *Composer Jerry Goldsmith (seated) with Brent Spiner, producer Rick Berman and Patrick Stewart.*

Academy Award-winning composer Jerry Goldsmith was chosen to create the musical score for *Star Trek: First Contact*. A veteran of *Star Trek* movies and television, Goldsmith created the musical theme for *Star Trek: The Motion Picture*, which later found itself reworked into the main title music for both *Star Trek: The Next Generation* and *Star Trek V: The Final Frontier*. For *First Contact*, Goldsmith wrote some brand new music for the opening titles, which he describes as "a very noble theme." The familiar theme from *The Next Generation* was also worked into the score in various places throughout the film, and can be heard over the end credits. As Goldsmith explains, "The end credits are a combination of both the new and the old theme." Elsewhere in the score, Goldsmith worked in other recognisable musical strains. "I quoted the old Klingon theme from *The Motion*

Picture for Worf when he comes on," he says. "I believe in using identifiable material. I think that's what makes a series successful musically. That's why the James Bond pictures worked so well with the John Barry scores — that signature was always there. So I stuck those in whenever I could. The audience will identify with it. Maybe not your average audience, but I think those that really like *Star Trek* will recognise all these musical motifs."

Three weeks were allotted for scoring *First Contact*, and Jerry Goldsmith says he was given a free hand to compose exactly what he wanted: "I was left pretty much to myself on it." He feels that the results of his endeavours combine with good storytelling to make this the finest *Star Trek* film to date: "This picture has more action in it. I think it's the best one of all. It has a spiritual theme. It has nice relationships and quite a bit of suspense." But how does one score for Borg? "Well, they're more high tech," he says, "so the music is more high tech for them, more electronics, a little bit more avant-garde." As for their leader: "It's a very sensuous Borg, the Borg Queen, so you have a sensuous, high tech sound. It was very interesting to do."

Goldsmith's long association with *Star Trek* in the cinema and on television also includes the aforementioned score for *The Final Frontier* and the theme for *Star Trek: Voyager*. "They're all a ball to do," he says. "I have a great deal of fun doing these. They're very romantic. They're a broad palette for me to work with. It's very melodic, and it's very operatic."

Jerry Goldsmith is one of the most respected composers working in the field today. He won an Academy Award in 1976 for Best Original Score for *The Omen*, and has been nominated fifteen times for the films *Star Trek: The Motion Picture*, *Basic Instinct*, *Hoosiers* (aka *Best Shot*), *Chinatown*, *Under Fire*, *Poltergeist*, *Patton*, *The Boys from Brazil*, *Papillon*, *The Wind and the Lion*, *Planet of the Apes*, *The Sand Pebbles*, *A Patch of Blue* and *Freud*. His recent film credits include *The Ghost and the Darkness*, *Executive Decision*, *Powder*, *City Hall*, *First Knight*, *Congo*, *The River Wild*, *I.Q.*, *The Shadow*, *Bad Girls*, *Angie*, *Malice*, *Six Degrees of Separation*, *Dennis the Menace*, *Rudy*, *The Vanishing* and many more. For television, the prolific Goldsmith won Emmy Awards for Best Score for *QB VII*, *The Red Pony*, *Masada* and *Babe*, and for the main title theme for *Star Trek: Voyager*. He also wrote the classic theme music for *The Man from U.N.C.L.E.*. ■

This page:
For the Borg, Goldsmith created a high tech, avant-garde sound.

THE CAST

Captain Jean-Luc Picard	Patrick Stewart
Commander William Riker	Jonathan Frakes
Lieutenant Commander Data	Brent Spiner
Lieutenant Commander Geordi La Forge	LeVar Burton
Lieutenant Commander Worf	Michael Dorn
Dr. Beverly Crusher	Gates McFadden
Commander Deanna Troi	Marina Sirtis
Lily Sloane	Alfre Woodard
Zefram Cochrane	James Cromwell
The Borg Queen	Alice Krige

THE FILM-MAKERS

Music by	Jerry Goldsmith
Co-producer	Peter Lauritson
Costume Designer	Deborah Everton
Special Animation and Visual Effects by	Industrial Light & Magic
Film Editor	John W. Wheeler, A.C.E.
Production Designer	Herman Zimmerman
Director of Photography	Matthew F. Leonetti, ASC
Executive Producer	Martin Hornstein
Story by	Rick Berman & Brannon Braga & Ronald D. Moore
Screenplay by	Brannon Braga & Ronald D. Moore
Produced by	Rick Berman
Directed by	Jonathan Frakes

(Credits are tentative as of 10 October and subject to change.)